IN THIS ISSUE

1 FROM THE DESK OF THE PRESIDENT

5 AN INTERVIEW WITH JOE FOSTER, FOUNDER OF REEBOK
CHRIS O'BYRNE

17 NONPROFIT OF THE MONTH: HYDRO WITH HOPE
WILL BLACK

20 CHALLENGERS AND ECOSYSTEMS IN BUSINESS
SAAR BEN-ATTAR

32 THE TRANSFORMATIVE POWER OF PUBLIC SPEAKING
KEN BURKE

47 DRIVING THE FUTURE OF E-LEARNING WITH MICROCASTING
KEN BURKE

55 USING INTERROGATION TECHNIQUES FOR BUSINESS GROWTH
DANIEL HAMMOND

67 AI IN MARKETING: HOW TO OUTSMART THE COMPETITION
CHRIS O'BYRNE

PIVOT Magazine

Founder and President
Jason Miller

Editor-in-Chief
Chris O'Byrne

Design
JETLAUNCH.net

Advertising
Chris O'Byrne

Webmaster
Joel Phillips

Editor
Laura West

Cover Design
Debbie O'Byrne

Cover Photographer
Jonna Persson

Copyright © 2023 PIVOT

ISBN: 979-8-89079-079-8

LETTER FROM THE EDITOR

At Pivot Magazine, we're dedicated to fueling the entrepreneurial spirit, and it's a privilege to feature Joe Foster, the founder of Reebok, in our latest issue. From the early days of shaping a nascent industry to creating a global brand, Joe's journey is a study in persistence, innovation, and belief in one's vision.

Joe's story is not just about building a brand; it's a lesson in turning adversities into opportunities and redefining an industry. Our conversation with Joe was a deep dive into the essence of entrepreneurship, filled with wisdom for anyone aspiring to make a lasting impact in their field. He embodies the spirit of what we celebrate at Pivot—the journey, the challenges, and the triumphs of making a mark in the business world.

In our discussion, Joe's insights emerged as timeless lessons for today's entrepreneurs. He emphasized the importance of being in the trenches with your team, identifying unmet market needs, and being agile enough to pivot direction swiftly. His approach to business, combining perseverance with a keen eye for white spaces, is a blueprint for modern entrepreneurial success.

Joe's story is more than a historical narrative; it's a guide for navigating the complexities of today's market, highlighting the importance of innovation, customer engagement, and storytelling in building a brand. As we share his journey, we hope it ignites a spark in our readers, encouraging the next generation of entrepreneurs to forge their paths of success, innovation, and impactful legacy.

Chris O'Byrne

FROM THE DESK OF THE PRESIDENT

At Pivot Magazine, we're on a mission to fuel the fire of entrepreneurs everywhere. We aim to be the spark that ignites innovative ideas and the wind that fans them into flames of success. Each issue is crafted to inspire, inform, and empower those who dare to dream and do. We celebrate the trailblazers and the visionaries who redefine what's possible in the business landscape, offering insights and stories that transform challenges into triumph.

In keeping with our tradition of excellence, we are thrilled to feature a very special guest in our latest issue. Joe Foster, the founder of Reebok, graces our pages with his remarkable story. Joe isn't just a figurehead in the business world; he's a pioneer who reimagined the athletic footwear industry and built a brand that has become a household name. His journey from humble beginnings to global success is a testament to the power of persistence, innovation, and the unwavering belief in one's vision.

Having the opportunity to interview Joe Foster was a highlight of my career. It's not every day that you get to have a conversation with someone whose life's work has influenced countless others, someone who has faced down the giants of industry and emerged victorious. Joe's insights are like a masterclass in entrepreneurship. They don't just skim the surface; they dive deep into the heart of what it means to build something enduring and transformative. His experiences, from the early struggles to the seismic shifts he navigated in the market, are rich with wisdom for anyone looking to leave their mark on the world.

As I talked with Joe, I couldn't help but feel honored to help his story reach a new generation of business leaders. His words are a powerful reminder that success is not just about the destination; it's about the journey, the people you meet along the way, and the lives you touch. Joe Foster isn't just special to entrepreneurs and businesspeople; he inspires anyone who understands that the biggest risks often lead to the greatest rewards.

* * *

As I talked with Joe, it became clear that his journey was paved with key business lessons that any entrepreneur could learn. Joe spoke of challenges as opportunities in disguise, urging that when a door seems to close, an often overlooked window might already be open. He impressed upon me the importance of resilience, which turns setbacks into comebacks. He shared how critical it is to listen—to the market, your customers, and sometimes, the silent hum of potential where no one else is looking.

Joe's recounting of the "white space"—those uncharted areas or market needs no one addresses—was particularly striking. He explained how Reebok carved out its niche in an Adidas-dominated world. When everyone else was busy outfitting soccer players, Reebok looked toward runners and aerobics enthusiasts. They filled a gap with a product that spoke directly to a growing community. It was about identifying and being brave enough to meet a need, even when it meant stepping away from the tried and true.

According to Joe, innovation and adaptability were the lifeblood of Reebok's success. He emphasized that to stay relevant, a business must evolve with its environment. When aerobics burst onto the scene, Reebok didn't just join the trend; they led it with innovative products that changed the game. Joe's approach was to anticipate change, to stay ahead of the curve, rather than scrambling behind it. He showed that the ability to adapt isn't just a survival skill—it's the hallmark of a thriving business.

Our conversation showed that Joe Foster's experiences aren't just relics of a bygone era. They are timeless reminders that in business, as in life, the only constant is change, and the only appropriate response is to innovate and adapt.

* * *

In our chat, Joe wasn't just recounting the past but mapping out a blueprint for the modern entrepreneur. His wisdom is timeless. He spoke of perseverance, vision, and the grit required in today's fast-paced business environment. It was clear that the lessons he learned in building Reebok are the same lessons today's startups need to hear. The landscape has changed, but the mountains one must climb in business are just as steep.

Joe's approach to business reshapes modern practices and leadership. He showed that a leader isn't just someone who makes decisions from an office chair but is in the trenches with their team, looking for those white spaces. His strategy of being on the ground, understanding customer needs, and pivoting the company's direction accordingly is the playbook for today's leaders operating in an era where markets shift overnight. His leadership style—open, adaptive, and always learning—prefigures the agile management that's become essential for any company aiming to innovate.

In our discussion, the impact of Joe's methodology was unmistakable. It's a framework that builds a culture of innovation, a habitat where creativity and courage drive progress. This approach is instrumental for today's businesses, which must navigate an ever-changing sea of consumer trends, technological advancements, and global shifts. His narrative isn't just a piece of history; it's a compass for today's business voyagers, guiding them through the unpredictable waters of the 21st-century marketplace.

* * *

When I think about what readers can gain from Joe Foster's insights, I'm reminded of the countless entrepreneurs I've met searching for that spark—that piece of wisdom that ignites their path to success. Joe's story offers just that. His insights provide more than just strategies; they offer a mindset. A mindset to see beyond the immediate

hurdles and view the long game, to recognize the potential in the quiet corners of the market, and to understand that real success is built on a foundation of genuine passion and hard work.

Joe Foster's influence on the entrepreneurial landscape is profound and enduring. His approach to business, his understanding of the market, and his ability to innovate are lessons that continue to resonate in boardrooms and startup garages alike. Joe's legacy is found in the way we think about branding, customer engagement, and creating products that don't just sell but tell a story. His journey underscores the importance of adapting to change, being fearless in the face of adversity,

and always moving forward, even when the path isn't clear.

Sharing Joe Foster's story with the readers of Pivot Magazine has been a privilege. Stories like his remind us why we are in business in the first place— to make an impact, innovate, and leave a mark on the world. Joe's narrative is a testament to the fact that with the right mix of tenacity, foresight, and a willingness to take risks, it's possible to turn a dream into a legacy. As we bring his story to you, I hope it sparks a flame of inspiration, lighting the way for the next generation of entrepreneurs to write their own stories of success.

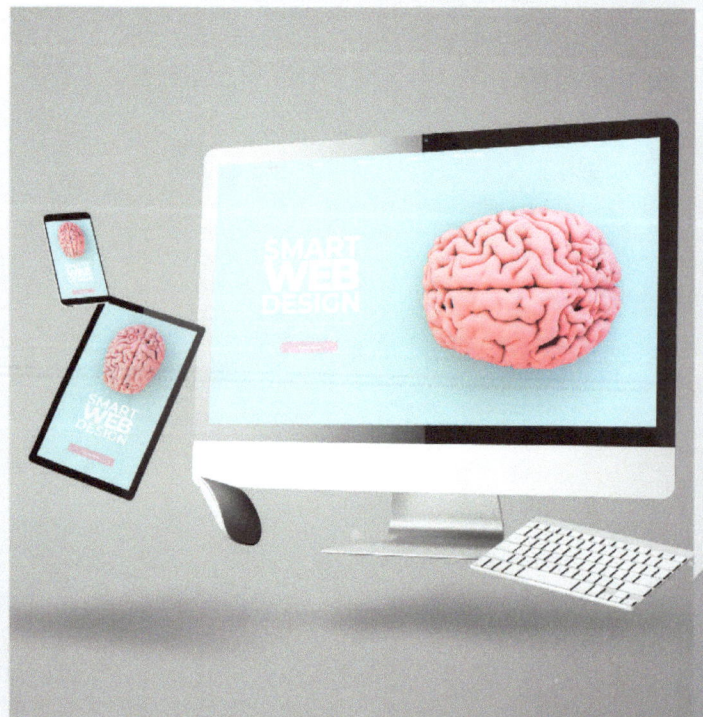

AN INTERVIEW WITH JOE FOSTER, FOUNDER OF REEBOK

Chris O'Byrne

What are one or two stories from your childhood that shaped who you are today?

Joe Foster

My most significant childhood memory is from 1943 when I was eight. This was during World War II. Like during COVID, travel was restricted, and there were no streetlights. I had already experienced four years of war by that point, and growing up in those conditions made it feel like a normal part of life, with many unique experiences.

Unable to go anywhere, I participated in a local eighty-yard race and emerged as the victor. This victory was greatly aided by a significant advantage I had—my grandfather, the founder of J.W. Foster. In 1904, he held three world records for his bike track shoes, having invented the spike track shoe. He even crafted shoes for the iconic athletes featured in *Chariots of Fire.* Although he passed away in 1933, before my birth in 1935, his legacy lived on. In 1943, I used his spiked shoes, securing my win.

Imagine this: Spike track shoes in 1943, and I was the only kid with them. I won the race but can't decide if it was cheating or my shoe advantage. When I went to collect my prize, I was handed a dictionary. At eight years old, I wondered, *Where's the football? What can I do with a dictionary?* At the time, I didn't know it was an American dictionary, specifically Webster's. Later, I discovered the differences in spellings compared to UK English, and this memory became quite significant in my life.

Another vivid memory is from our time in Bolton, near Manchester. Manchester was a prime target due to its docks and industry. We had a view extending eight to ten miles to Manchester from our upstairs rooms. We would hear the sirens during air raids and know the raids were happening. For about six months, we sought refuge in our shelter, but as time passed, everyone grew tired of it because Bolton wasn't a significant target. We stopped going into the shelters and would watch from our bedroom windows as the flames glowed red in the distance from Manchester. These memories, particularly the air-raid alarms and the clear sirens, have stayed with me over the years. These are two of my enduring memories from my youth.

We had a shortage of teachers because they served in the army. Consequently, my first ten years of life were marked by limited access to education. My mother played a massive role in filling the gap, and we had a few women who worked as teachers at that time. However, it was challenging to replace everyone. We might have attended school occasionally, but the schools had been repurposed during the war as air-raid posts and safe havens in case of emergencies. Formal education was almost nonexistent, but we had books and my mother's guidance, which allowed me to learn and read, so I managed reasonably well. It wasn't until I was around ten that we began to receive a more formal education and return to school.

Chris O'Byrne

You mentioned that the American dictionary was important later in your life. How did that become important to you?

Joe Foster

In 1958, my brother and I decided to leave the family business, J W Foster & Sons. Unfortunately, our grandfather, the founder, had passed away before my birth. The company was then under the control of my father and uncle, who were engaged in a bitter feud reminiscent of the story of Adolf and Rudolf Dassler. While Rudolf wisely left to establish Puma, the Foster family continued their infighting, leading the company to a decline.

Jeff, my older brother, and I recognized the situation and decided to confront our father. We told him something needed to change. However, he could only respond, "Joe, when I'm gone, and your uncle is gone, this company will be yours. You can do what you like with it then." It was obvious to Jeff and me that we didn't want our father to die. We weren't seeking that outcome. But the way things were going, the company would deteriorate long before he did. Would he listen to our concerns? No, and we couldn't understand why. Perhaps it had something to do with their experiences during the two World Wars, or maybe they were content with a comfortable living and didn't want to change.

Adidas and Puma had entered the market, with Adidas dominating the soccer sector. We felt the urgency to act. In my grandfather's era, he supplied boots and training shoes to all the major football and soccer teams—a whopping ninety teams—but we had lost all those partnerships. Jamie Foster's business had suffered. In response, my brother Jeff and I decided to leave. We set up our own company and secured a small factory, naming it Mercury Sport Footballer. We were happy with that, successfully selling shoes and making money.

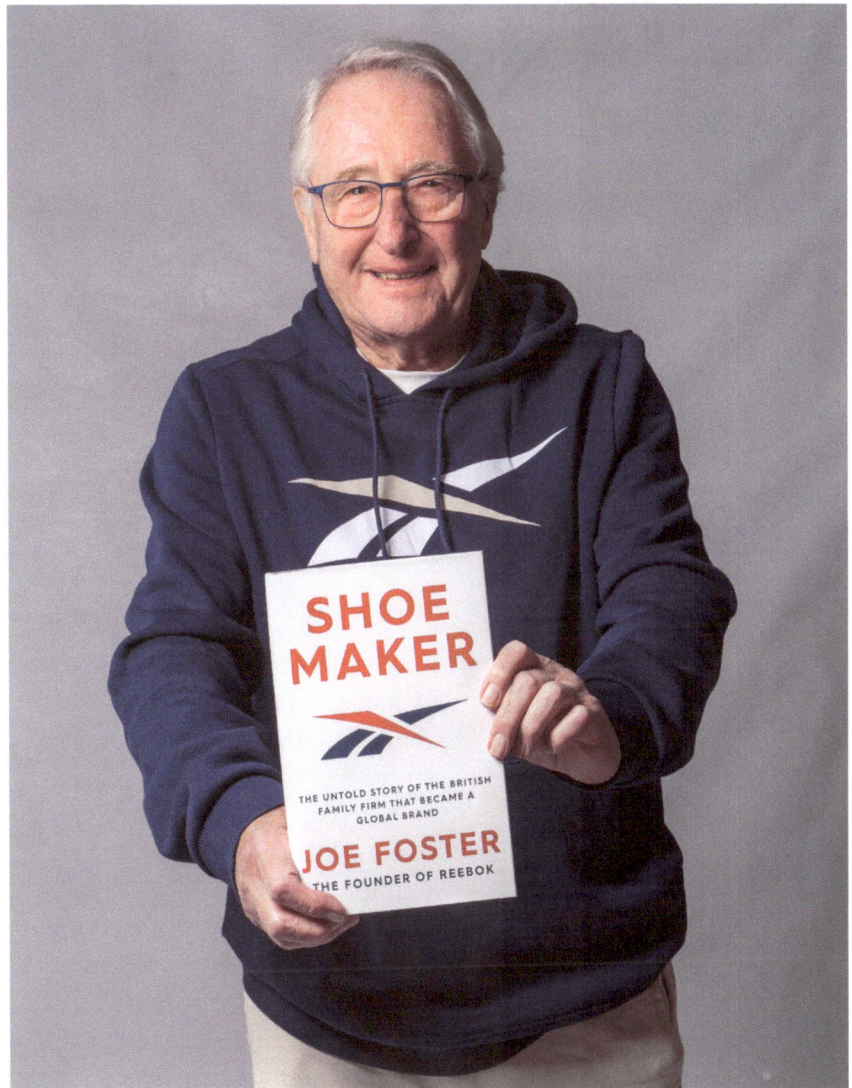

Our accountant advised, "Joe, you better register your name." What? We were taken aback, asking, "Why would we need to register our name? We are Mercury." Looking back, we were quite naive.

Given that Jeff and I share the same initials, it would have been a straightforward step if we had chosen to establish ourselves as J.W. Foster. No registration would have been necessary for your name. However, that would have meant direct competition with the parent company, something we wanted to avoid. So, we stuck with the name Mercury.

"So, what do we register?" we asked. Our accountant's warning was clear: If we don't register, someone else might decide to make Mercury shoes, leading to a potential legal dispute over the name. To avoid that, we decided to register it. He provided us with the contact information of a patent agent, and I went to see him to initiate the registration process. After conducting his checks, the patent agent returned within a week with the news that "Mercury" had already been preregistered by the British Shoe Corporation, a massive company.

We wondered what our options were. The patent agent told us that he had contacted them, and they were willing to sell us the name. That sounded promising. We asked, "How much do they want?" Their asking price was £1,000. In those days, we had established an entire factory for just £250, including machinery and all; £1,000 seemed steep, and the bank wasn't inclined to provide such a loan. Repaying it and even securing the opportunity to borrow that sum was daunting. We concluded that it wasn't a viable option for us.

He suggested taking them to court since they weren't using the name, which could allow us to claim it. I inquired about the cost of pursuing the legal route, to which he replied, "About a thousand pounds." I quickly realized it was a futile endeavor and not something we were willing to pursue.

On a nice day in early May with the sun shining, he pointed to a sign that read *Kodak*. I asked him about it, and he explained that Kodak was their invented

name, not one chosen from a list. He advised me that creating one from scratch was the best approach to choosing a name. He added, "Don't just bring me one name; come up with ten." I felt overwhelmed at the thought of generating ten names, as finding even one good name can be challenging. I told him that to accomplish this, we needed to be deeply passionate and committed to the task, and we had to love what we were doing.

The lawyer's role was simply to confirm the availability of names. I went back. Afterward, we brainstormed around a table and considered various names, including Cougar and Falcon. These names seemed to align well with the sports theme: Cougar Sport and Falcon Sport. We also explored other animal and bird-related names. During

this brainstorming session, my Webster's American dictionary, which I preferred for the letter R, sat nearby. I opened it to the letter R and quickly came across "Reebok," defined as a small South African gazelle. Considering our company's focus on running, "Gazelle" seemed like a perfect fit. It immediately rose to the top of our list, and with that, we had our ten names, including Reebok.

I returned to the patent agent with the list of ten names, making it clear that we were particularly fond of "Reebok." Despite our preference, he completed the necessary process, which took about two weeks. Eventually, he said, "Joe, you got your wish. 'Reebok' is the most suitable choice." However, he noted a couple of problems—phonetically, "Reebok" could be confused with

"Reebock," and there was another company named "Reebok" that specialized in women's underwear. The latter was less concerning since they were also patent agents, and the similarity in names was not a significant problem. That's how we ended up with "Reebok."

The registrar initially placed us in the B-section of the register, explaining that he could only do so. We were unaware of the register's existence until about a month prior. We didn't mind an A-section or B-section, as we couldn't fathom anything using Reebok skin for sports footwear. Ten years later, the registrar moved us to the A-section because Reebok had become widely recognized as a sports brand, causing concern. That's the essence of the story.

Chris O'Byrne

Who were some of your most important influences or mentors along your journey?

Joe Foster

The words "mentors" and "influencers" may have been in my vocabulary, but they weren't commonly used in business back then. Nowadays, it's all about influencers and mentors. We actively sought opportunities to attend college and connect with people. Going to college was a good thing, and in a sense, those influencers became our mentors,

teaching us the art of shoemaking beyond our prior knowledge of athletic footwear. They imparted valuable insights in that regard.

Within a fifteen-mile radius, there was a hub for the football industry, primarily focusing on sneakers and budget-friendly shoes. One notable individual in the vicinity was John Willy Johnson, who operated a small shoe factory. He was content earning just sixpence, about ten cents, for each pair of shoes he produced. Despite the modest profit margin, he accumulated substantial wealth by manufacturing many shoes.

Today, the UK's footwear industry is in decline as more production moves to the Far East, where products are available at less than half the price while maintaining high quality. In regions like Northampton and the Langtree area, where our factory was located, businesses were shutting down at an alarming rate, leading to frequent auctions, sometimes even monthly.

I used to attend those auctions out of necessity, as we were short on funds. The best part was buying a sewing machine for just two pounds; it was fantastic. John Willy Johnson also frequented the auctions. He always sat in the front row and rarely made a bid on anything. However, when the auctioneer couldn't find any takers for many odds and ends, he would look at John, who

simply nodded, and it was his. This piqued my curiosity because he bought every piece of rubbish you could imagine. He was the guy who cleared out all the odds and ends while most others were buying machines.

Once, I bought a lot of leather and rented a van to transport it. I loaded the van, although clearly too much for it. The van felt more like a speedboat riding a wave as I drove. Naturally, a police officer pulled me over because I exceeded the weight limit. I had to go through the process of getting the load weighed and paying the fine and associated penalties.

The next time I spoke with John, I mentioned my encounter with the police when transporting the leather. I wasn't sure if I made any money on that purchase due to that incident. John reassured me, saying, "Joe, whatever you buy, just let me know. My team handles clearance after the sale, and they'll pick up your items, too." Given that he was only fifteen miles away, he added, "And they'll deliver it to you." I expressed my gratitude, thanking John for his assistance.

Then, John proposed a more efficient plan. He suggested, "Instead of both of us driving separately for sixty to seventy miles, why don't we carpool?" I agreed to this idea, saying, "Fair enough, John. I'll pick you up." However, he had already seen my car and said, "You come over, park your car, and we'll go in mine." When we met, I asked John, "What do you do with all those items you pick up at these sales?" I was curious about the outcome.

John had a large, old mill with a warehouse filled with various items, including stuffed crocodiles, birds, and more. He showed me a machine called a "pounding-up machine" that could remove wrinkles from the leather. I asked John if I could rent or buy the machine, but he refused both options, saying I could have it and return it when done. I expressed my gratitude, and he even offered to have his team deliver and set up the machine on our production line.

This wasn't the only instance. John offered me machines numerous times, and I believe we ended up with around five or six. He seemed to have a knack for knowing what equipment I could use. He stands out as the most impressive when discussing mentors or people who offered assistance. His genuine nature and generosity with his time and resources left a lasting impact. Unfortunately, he passed away a few years ago at the age of ninety, as he was much older than me. I'm only eighty-eight, still a junior in comparison.

Chris O'Byrne

A young man. What are some of the most valuable lessons you've learned over the years?

Joe Foster

First, it's crucial to assemble a team that takes ownership and embraces the identity of Reebok. Team members should not focus on themselves but on being part of the Reebok team. Listening to others is essential. While I introduced certain aspects like silhouettes, the name, and the logo to the company, building a team was paramount. They should proudly say, "We are Reebok. I am Reebok," and genuinely feel a part of the brand.

Building a team was critical, and I had challenges with egos. If I identified anyone with an ego issue, I would kindly ask them to move on. Ego-driven behavior was not the right fit; we needed people eager to be part of the team. Therefore, team building was probably the most significant aspect. Additionally, honesty and integrity were essential when dealing with the team. If you have that, people trust you. Building trust with your team is crucial because if they trust you, like John Willey did with us, they'll be willing to help, and people generally want to contribute.

When asked about the three most important aspects of

building and running a company, I'd say:

1. It must be enjoyable. If you're not having fun, it will be challenging.
2. Make it even more enjoyable.
3. It should be a real hoot, a source of tremendous fun. When it's this enjoyable, everyone on the team is also having a great time. They don't even realize they started at 6 a.m., and it's now 10 p.m.; they don't want to go home. You're a family.

You build a culture around a tangible product with three dimensions, like a shoe. Apparel, lacking this depth, relies on people wearing it. We emphasize our achievements and foster a winning culture, particularly in sports, where success is visible and distinct from routine tasks. Building, listening, and forming a cohesive team are so important.

Chris O'Byrne

A lot of businesses today are completely online. What do you suggest for building that team culture when nobody is even in the same room?

Joe Foster

I've never had a problem with this because I started before computers, smartphones, and the internet. We used to sell via mail order and magazine advertisements, employing direct

Credit: Forbes Mexico

marketing and sales methods. In essence, we were doing what's happening today, but we were doing it through a different medium. If you're doing what's happening today, just through a different medium, the key remains to build effective teams and create excitement.

Today, influencers play a crucial role. It's a completely different landscape. When we got into aerobics, Jane Fonda purchased and wore Reebok on TV, and her fitness videos had a significant impact. However, such an approach wouldn't

work in today's world. Times have changed, and I'm currently collaborating with someone who has authored a book titled *Start, Scale, Exit, Repeat.*

It's a brilliant, weighty book, and the author acknowledges learning from me. We've been doing university interviews, and they often ask about our exit plan. We didn't have one; our goal was to make a living and be successful. So, am I an entrepreneur or a brand builder? We certainly built a brand, and while being an entrepreneur is part of that, it's not the same

as someone like Colin, a serial entrepreneur. Today, it's common for people to start something, make money, and start anew. Things have evolved, especially here in America, which I love.

Some guys sell something for $30 million, and you wonder if you need a billion. It can be addictive, the idea of starting and scaling. Not much has changed; it's just the language and methods that have evolved have changed. It still boils down to people, ideas, and establishing a credible brand.

To establish credibility for your brand, in our case, it was through gold medals that influenced people. Similarly, supplying a soccer team can influence the sports brand world. It's still about understanding how people become aware of your brand and want to purchase it. In 1895, my grandfather founded his company and invented the Spike running shoe. By 1904, he had provided his shoes to athletes like Alfred Shrubb, who astonishingly broke three world records in one race in Glasgow.

After Alfred Shrubb's success, the strategy shifted to influencers, who were given shoes to wear and share their positive experiences with commentators and article writers. This generated great reviews and endorsements. As we expanded, we delved into the history of GIDB, particularly my grandmother's contributions since we were local to where he started his business. In one historical advertisement, we discovered a bold claim: "If you don't believe that Foster's spikes are the best you've ever worn, we'll give you 100 pounds."

Thinking about the early twentieth century, offering £100 as a guarantee was equivalent to roughly £10,000 today, a substantial amount of money in those days. His advertising strategy included showcasing top runners who had won gold medals while wearing his shoes.

Influence has evolved somewhat today, where it's often more open but may involve payments. You must figure out how to effectively incorporate influencers into your business.

Chris O'Byrne

What is something in business that most people don't see?

Joe Foster

Many pursue business without considering whether they'll enjoy it or find it fulfilling. Fun and passion are crucial because the commitment is 24/7; it needs to be on your mind and shared with your team. Today, some focus on starting, scaling, exiting, and repeating, but success often requires a genuine love for what you do.

It's about finding what you consider fun. For some, like the person we're talking about, the thrill is in the game itself, not just the product. You must decide what aspect is enjoyable for you, whether it's building something for the long term or another aspect. In our case, the Reebok legacy stretches back to my grandfather in 1895; now, in 2023, it's been 128 years. While Reebok has changed, it's coming back, although Adidas bought it. However, Adidas primarily sought the assets and integrated them rather than focusing on the growth of Reebok.

Reebok endured and was sold to ABG two years ago. The problem with Adidas was their failure to maintain Reebok as an independent entity; they integrated everything into one system. The separation process feels as intricate as performing surgery.

It's taken a few years, but ABG's notable strength lies in its extensive global distribution. They've formed partnerships with various entities to expand the brand. During our recent trip to India earlier this year, we connected with a new Indian team that secured a remarkable forty-year license, reflecting a significant commitment.

ABG has a strategic approach, and we've secured valuable partnerships. ABG paid $2.5 billion for a company initially valued at $3.6 billion but is estimated to be worth less. The reason is their CEO, Jamie Salter, who owns Jack O'Neal's brand and holds a 15 percent stake in ABG. Shaquille O'Neal, who is closely connected to ABG, expressed a strong interest in acquiring Reebok every time he visited, making the purchase a promising move.

In business, you must have a genuine passion, not just a casual interest. That deep desire makes you invest extra time and thought, not just money. It's about making people believe in your vision, and delivering when they trust you is vital. If you believe in your vision, others will, too. Having someone like Shaquille O'Neal, now appointed as the president of basketball, is exciting, especially as Reebok is making a strong return to basketball, which I love.

He believes in aiming high, currently targeting the number three spot but ultimately striving for the top position, even though Nike seems quite distant. Dreaming big is essential for achieving remarkable goals. This approach applies to any business. How successful do you want to be? While financial success is one aspect, industries like sports demand a deeper passion and commitment beyond just making money. It's about being in love with what you do, especially in industries where visibility is key.

Reebok is back on a winning trajectory, and it's wonderful to see. This year, Julie and I have had the opportunity to visit Reebok teams in Australia, Singapore, Dubai, and India. We've also previously traveled to Panama and Canada to connect with the Reebok teams in those regions.

I'm not involved with Reebok, but as a founder, it's important to remember that a founder's role remains constant. CEOs and other team members can change, but the founder is a unique and irreplaceable presence.

Chris O'Byrne

Throughout your journey, can you recall a specific moment when you gained a deep understanding of a particular aspect of business as you progressed and were able to reflect and say, "Okay, now I get it"?

Joe Foster

We constantly took steps to grow and scale our business, aiming to see how far we could go. Breaking into the American market was a pivotal moment. After spending eleven years trying at NSGA and facing numerous failures, our breakthrough came when we earned five-star ratings for three of our shoes from *Runner's World*. That was a turning point because it attracted significant attention and established our brand in the market. Five-star ratings proved to be a powerful influence.

Our strategy was always about finding untapped opportunities, or white space. We needed to discover areas no one had ventured into in a market dominated by giants like Nike, Adidas, and Puma. We identified the running and athletics sectors in the UK, particularly through our affiliation with the Three A's Handbook. This handbook connected us with over 300 clubs, allowing us to appoint around 250 Reebok agents. Consequently, we successfully established our presence in that market. With that space secured,

we continued to look for new opportunities and expand our footprint.

We identified the rugby league as an untapped opportunity in the UK, especially in northern England. Knocking on doors and providing a few pairs of boots was often enough to enter this space. However, when we expanded to America, it was a different challenge. It wasn't about finding white space but about a much larger market. How do you scale and grow in a market like that? Do you introduce more products or diversity into football? (Adidas dominated soccer.) Alternatively, do you expand your geographical territory? We opted to expand internationally, capitalizing on the UK's Commonwealth connections, enabling us to enter markets like Canada, New Zealand, Australia, and India, where there was demand for English products due to the common language.

I had connections like Frank Ryan, a Yale University coach, when we entered the American market. However, he was getting older and wasn't keen on working with Reebok. However, I understood the coach held a prestigious position in every college and university, and they were instrumental in the sports world. It took eleven years, but I knew entering the American market was worth the effort due to its size. We eventually made our way in through RunNin and grew into a $9 million business.

Back then, as a relatively unknown $9 million business, we were just a small player in the vast running market. Then, the opportunity in aerobics emerged. Our tech rep in Los Angeles heard from his wife about these energetic exercise-to-music classes, and he realized we could tap into this. It was called aerobics, and he observed that some participants wore sneakers while others went barefoot. The idea of creating a dedicated shoe for aerobics struck him, and that was our white space.

He wanted the aerobics shoe made from simple white glove leather, and at that time, we had the Union Jack on the side of our shoes. Shortly after bringing Paul Fireman on as our USA distributor, he raised concerns about our Roadster logo resembling the Union Jack. He thought it would be costly to establish the Roadster in America and suggested using the Union Jack instead, as it was universally recognizable. I was hesitant because I knew we'd face backlash in the UK since the shoes were manufactured in the Far East. However, I agreed to make the change. We put the Union Jack on each shoe and even on the box lid. Retailers began stacking these boxes in a pyramid with a shoe on each one, which became a popular display. It caught on, but we faced around a dozen court cases in the UK from those who believed we couldn't do this since the shoes weren't made there.

We argued that our shoes were designed in the UK and received a royalty on every shoe, so we should be allowed to use the Union Jack. We pointed out that even British Airways had the Union Jack on their planes' tails. The legal battles led to some minor fines, around one pound each, and eventually, we agreed with the authorities to pay around 5,000 pounds to end the dispute. Despite having "Made in Korea" tags on the side of every shoe, we persevered.

Indeed, the shoes were made in South Korea. They were successful in America, but I did not know that Arthold had requested glove leather because glove leather is traditionally used for gloves, not shoes. It's delicate, like a piece of paper that can be easily torn. As a result, the shoes started falling apart. In any other country or location except Los Angeles, USA, we might have faced failure and been discarded. We could have been dismissed, but the girls loved those shoes so much that they didn't mind if they only lasted four weeks or less.

When I realized the shoes were falling apart, I asked what could be done to address this issue. The solution was to line them with nylon to add strength, but I pointed out that this would hinder breathability, a crucial feature of leather. The marketing team devised a creative solution: punched holes in the front to allow the shoes to breathe. This was a valuable lesson for me in the power of marketing. Reebok's introduction of soft leather was a game-changer in America. Reebok made soft leather popular, and now, everyone uses it because there's no need to break in the shoes.

Before the introduction of soft leather, many shoes required so much breaking in that they were almost worn out by the time they became comfortable. This transition was challenging. I recall an agency, possibly SolGold, running an advertisement when we entered the tennis market with our soft shoes. The ad read something to the effect of *If you don't believe that the Reebok tennis shoe is the best you've ever worn, we'll replace your shoes and give you a can of balls*. The tagline was "Reebok puts his balls on the lines."

A brand should have a sense of fun and be able to appreciate the lighter side of life. The move into soft leather shoes for tennis was a vast white space that propelled us from a $9 million business to a $900 million one in just four years. It was a game-changer, and at that time, we even surpassed Adidas and Nike to become number one in the late 1980s.

We transitioned from primarily a running company to a women's company, thanks to the success of the aerobic shoes. Initially designed for women and available in women's sizes, they took off, and soon, men wanted a piece of the action. This led us to develop various models for aerobics, training, and other purposes. As we grew in size and influence, we expanded into other sports like basketball, football, and even baseball. We focused on sports where the same shoe could be worn on the street, making it versatile and appealing to a broader audience.

Chris O'Byrne

What are some parting words of wisdom you have for us?

Joe Foster

It may not be wisdom and art, but the key is to have fun, build strong teams, enjoy interacting with people, and be a good listener. There are countless individuals out there with more ideas than you. I stepped back at age 55 because I recognized the importance of embracing the younger generation's fresh and innovative ideas. We need these new perspectives, even if some attempts fail. What's vital is being open to others' ideas and actively listening. That's the best advice I could offer people.

Also, take calculated risks; if you find that you're wrong, don't hesitate to change. The worst decision is not deciding at all. Regardless of which path you choose, making a decision is crucial, and if it turns out to be wrong, be willing to adapt and change course.

The same principle applies to the people who work for you. Encourage them to make decisions, even if they fear making the wrong ones. You can explore new avenues and chart a different course through these decisions. For example, Arto's decision to create aerobics shoes was initially wrong, but it could be changed. Eventually, we switched to a more substantial clothing leather, as glove leather is only one millimeter thick, and working on it can thin it down to 0.7 millimeters.

That's the beauty of inviting people to take initiative. I advised Paul Fireman not to learn how to make shoes because doing so can limit your ability to think differently. When you become a shoemaker, you start thinking like one, insisting on specific features, materials, and processes, and you end up making shoes like everybody else. To be innovative, you must be willing to change and explore new ideas. For instance, glove leather didn't initially work because it wasn't strong enough, but we kept working on the concept to create something that worked—and succeeded.

NONPROFIT OF THE MONTH: HYDRO WITH HOPE

WILL BLACK

The first thing every parent needs to hear when they learn that their child is one of the one million people in the US with hydrocephalus is simply, "This is not the end of the world." That's what Jeff Pearson of the Hydro With Hope Foundation likes to tell everyone. After all, here he is forty-six years later as a husband, father, and business owner. Most don't know that he had his first surgery at two weeks old, and that was at a time when he had to be born before diagnosis. We can tell in the first trimester, but for him forty-six years ago, it was done by measuring his head to body size.

Jeff was in the hospital one day, and on the other side of the curtain, a family was being given that dreadful news: Their beautiful baby had hydrocephalus, and it was the worst hour on what should have been one of the best days of their lives. He wanted to push through that curtain and hug them, talk with them, and let them know, "This is not the end of the world."

Instead, he started Hydro With Hope to let people know. They even have a show on the e360tv network called *Invisible Condition*, which as of mid-2023 had 7,000 viewers and growing.

It's not odd, as Jeff is a good-looking, charismatic man. He has good and bad days, too, but who doesn't? Most never know Jeff has hydrocephalus, and he inspires those around him looking for guidance. But he knows not knowing is the real fear.

"We simply created what we always wanted—collateral. Real-world, hard collateral." He did it in the form of a journal that parents can start, but their children can end up participating in and eventually finish.

But it's not enough. He continually creates so that families, parents, and even the children themselves can see life goes on and is, in fact, good.

Because Jeff is living it, more is coming in terms of his shows, his media content, and his life. He did not die that day, even though his family had to trust in the unknown, but it all turned out very well indeed. The main thing for him right now is the same as it was that day—he wishes he had ignored all protocol and had simply pushed the curtain aside. To give comfort, to share knowledge, and to say that he did and so will that child.

"This is just the beginning..."

CHALLENGERS AND ECOSYSTEMS IN BUSINESS

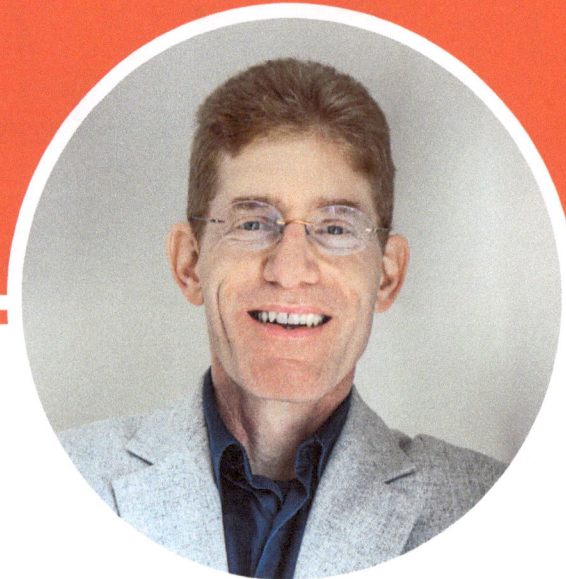

SAAR BEN-ATTAR

Chris O'Byrne:

Before we dig into what you're doing now, can you tell me about your background and what led you to where you are now?

Saar Ben-Attar:

I wish I could say this story unfolded in a straight line. I started my professional career while I was still at university. It was during the final year of my postgraduate degree. I was getting fairly bored and the only alternative to sitting in lectures was spending all my time by the beach. Cape-Town has some of the world's best beaches, but I felt I couldn't do that for long, certainly not for a year. I started looking for opportunities to do something different.

I have always loved speaking with people and hearing their stories. I reached out to the farming community in the area, which includes some of the most sophisticated wine growers, as well as hi-tech hydroponic and vertical farming operations. We ended up having philosophical discussions, about everything from irrigation solutions to management systems needed for the 21st Century. It was a wonderful time, getting to know them. I met some incredible people. I got loads of wine bottles of the best quality, as presents. I did that for a while. Then I got hired full-time by the company I was representing in my final year of study. I developed the entire province for them for about two years. I loved the interactions and networks. I didn't know the word ecosystem at that stage. Still, I appreciated the collective intelligence that people in the area had built and how they were helping each other become more productive and solve real problems.

I then spent a couple of years in manufacturing. I was ambitious about taking manufacturers from the emerging world, in some of the more industrialized African markets, Latin America, and the Middle East. I took those organizations to the US market. In the mid-1990's, that was largely unheard of, imports came in from China and India largely. Talk about challenging the status quo. Again, what fascinated me more than anything else were the connections that were built, and now these connections were across the ocean.

Suddenly, you had some of the most sophisticated organizations, such as Kmart and Target on the retail side, as well as some wholesaling organizations venturing into building their brands. They were creating strategic relationships with suppliers on the other side of the ocean.

I discovered two things during that growth experience. First, a wonderful collective of individuals who's shared insights brought about new solutions and created real innovations. For example, we were on the first global pilot, run by shipping company Maersk, for container tracking. Now, you can easily go online, click a few times, and know exactly where your containers are. In 1991, that wasn't the case pretty much anywhere in maritime shipping. I was immensely proud that we were chosen as one of the first companies for that container tracking pilot. Many technological and management innovations were now converging and becoming available to smaller firms, such as us. The world was becoming smaller.

Our clients didn't seem to care whether we were from South Africa, Mexico, Canada, Turkey, or other countries. They cared more that we shared an ambition with them. They cared that they could do something interesting with us. We started a series of conversations about what their brand could stand for. Could they create an experience for customers that the known name brands were not providing? Could they do it on their own? Even at a premium, rather than compete solely on price?

It was an incredible period. I met individuals and organizations that were ambitious, outgoing, *and thinking in global terms. We didn't have all the systems and governance in place yet, and we were still trying to figure out how to optimally route containers from point A to point B.*

I spent about seven years with that company. We had a terrific run and built a team I'm proud of to this day. Those were my formative years, as I came out of university and connected with people around new ideas.

Chris O'Byrne:

You have a unique perspective about the world, which I think has affected how you view business and make these connections and create these insights. You didn't have the typical view of business that you sell stuff, try to get people to buy it, and market it. Everything you just told me was encapsulating all of that. You used the term ecosystems, and that's how you see the world through this ecosystem lens. Can you explain a little more about what an ecosystem in business means and looks like?

Saar Ben-Attar:

What brought me to realising the power of ecosystems was seeking closer connection with others, who I was working with. Sometimes, it wasn't even my realization; others opened doors and asked why not. I came across the work of James E. Moore, who I believe coined the term ecosystems and made it into a management discipline, something that we could practically use and challenge how we could operate businesses differently. He started writing about ecosystems back in 1993. In 1998, he published his book, *The Death of Competition*. I remember the minute I picked up that book and started reading. I thought, *There's something different here*. The ideas behind it were compelling, and the narrative he was putting out as to the nature of competition changing irrevocably. We need to think about how we respond to such a seismic shift. That drew me into this field.

In the simplest of terms, an ecosystem, whether a biological ecosystem one finds in nature, a business ecosystem, or a social ecosystem among stakeholders who do not have a commercial interest in collaborating—you can boil down the definition to the following: An ecosystem is a collection of stakeholders working together toward a shared goal.

Unfortunately, the word ecosystem can be misused. It's one of the most widely used terms these days. If you do a Google search, you'll find millions of entries around the term ecosystem. However, if I take some of the hype away, there's real substance behind it, and James Moore hit the nail on the head when he spoke about it for the first time. The case for ecosystem is still here today. In many ways, we're

sitting on the cusp of ecosystems becoming the operating model, across industries.

There are a few features to an ecosystem, which distinguishes it from simply being a network of economic actors. First, there must be a shared goal that we are all working towards. This is more than simply agreeing to a number, say a revenue goal, something we could sell to the board. It's much more than that. It means a meeting of the minds. It means we share a mindset, and that we took the time to develop a coherent strategy for the ecosystem, where all parties benefit in some way. Without this, an ecosystem, however well designed, doesn't come to life.

The second feature that distinguishes an ecosystem from an alliance or bilateral partnership between two parties is that, in an ecosystem, we don't work to a rule. In other words, we don't have the dominant player managing or directing the other role players, imposing their (often slow) decision-making onto others. Now, I am not saying that there are no power dynamics in an ecosystem; of course there are. But, even if an organization and its leaders have good intentions of how the ecosystem should operate, one of the distinguishing features of any ecosystem is the fact that the ecosystem works along shared principles, not dominance.

There are ground rules and smart contracts to regulate boundaries between role players. Yet we allow the freedom for ecosystem role players to participate in the ecosystem, and that means they may find better ways for the ecosystem to create value. The ecosystem can then evolve, while new role players can join the ecosystem and more readily contribute their unique capabilities. That is where you will financial institutions, for example, partnering with a range of non-financial firms, or energy companies partnering with a host of digital players and others. Ecosystems are simply not hierarchical by design, and what we gain in this way is speed and scale, which are unmatched.

The third distinguishing feature of an ecosystem is that it allows for new forms of business and commercial models to take hold. This requires ecosystem governance to be in place and is one of an ecosystem's strongest and most enduring features. We begin with an idea of how the ecosystem should operate but then allow participating parties to find better ways. We may be solving for financial inclusion, for example, a huge problem in emerging countries as well as some developed markets. All we know is where we want to start.

An ecosystem is based on an organizing set of principles and a model within which different participating parties know where they start and allow themselves and others to evolve. That's how biological ecosystems work in nature. We may have started as a certain organism, that founded an ecosystem around them. In a natural ecosystem, organisms often take a few million years to evolve. However, business evolution can happen much faster. We can iterate and rediscover more quickly. Once you've done that, you find better solutions. If we could go back four and a half billion years and ask, "Will man rule the earth?" We wouldn't have been able to conceive of modern human beings looking at a single-cell organism. That's the power of ecosystems—their richness, innovation, and ability to bring different parties together toward a shared outcome.

Chris O'Byrne:

There's been a lot of talk over the last few years about self-managing companies. What is the connection between ecosystems and self-managing companies? Is a self-managing company one of the potential outcomes or iterations of the ecosystem model?

Saar Ben-Attar:

Ecosystems did not start in 1993 when James Moore wrote about it for the first time. Some of the organizing principles around ecosystems, includes self-managing teams, were being tested in the 1960s and at scale certainly by the 1970s. By the 1980s, people such as Tom Peters wrote best-selling books about these concepts.

There is a direct link between self-managing teams and the many ways organizations worldwide have been experimenting with ecosystems. What is different today is we can get self-managing teams to work with the power of technology, well beyond their immediate workspace. Self-managing teams can become the core of a growing ecosystem. This morning, for example, our team looked at a biomedical company out of China that is creating a global ecosystem with the advent of digital technologies and the ability to collaborate at scale and across great distances. We didn't have those solutions back in the 1970s. Now, we can use self-managing teams—on steroids—due to technology. We can create global impact with self-managing teams but do self-managing teams include the organizing principles of ecosystems? You bet. It's a great question. I'm so glad you asked me that.

Chris O'Byrne:

Please tell me about your company. What do you do, and how do you run your company?

Saar Ben-Attar:

My company is called Ascent Growth Partners. We started in 2016 in South Africa and opened our second office in Singapore during 2019. Just imagine, that was six months before the pandemic. None of us saw that coming. Beyond our core team, we have a very rich ecosystem of specialists, business partners and innovators, a network of capabilities one can rely on and, most importantly, challenge with.

Before we launched Ascent Growth Partners, we began conversations with potential clients about the challenges they were facing. Like many innovators, we just had an idea that we were seeing a recurring challenge, that these organizations couldn't solve on their own. They were recognizing that and looking for new partners. *The challenge was the ability to grow beyond their core business into new ecosystems.* For example, those kinds of ecosystems were being built around mobile technologies, from mobile financial services, electric mobility, to IoT solutions. Those organizations speaking to us saw the opportunity and were reaching out to people who could help them. However, there wasn't an organizing structure around these efforts. It was a bunch of experiments that no one could put their finger on. First, they had to sell the idea to their board. Second, they had to get funding for these ideas. And third, they struggled to measure the impact. In these new spaces, we couldn't just say, "You said you would do X, Have we achieved X?" They needed a new set of measures to understand how effective their ecosystem building efforts were.

When we speak about ecosystems, we begin to measure the impact, in a broader sense. How did the customer's life change? Who else benefited? Which ecosystem players can unlock economic value, which couldn't before? Could we participate with them, rather than narrowly measure our core business P&L? On average, we find that ecosystem strategies, which we help develop, can generate three to four times the impact than traditional business strategies.

In our work, we are often called in once a client is in the midst of transformation. They recognize the opportunity that lies beyond their core business, or their core business has irrevocably changed. Some even developed a vision of what they would like to achieve within a broader ecosystem.

Many have taken some bold steps and invested in digital technologies, at times have had consultants working with them, but now as they navigate the journey, the CEO and their leadership team would like a second opinion, they would like to confirm that no "navigational errors" were made. They would like an objective party taking a data-driven yet human-centered look at their business' growth path and bring new insights into their transition. In working together, they are able to shift their mindset, see the opportunity with a new pair of eyes. They develop new options, pathways to growth and are more receptive to new capabilities, which can be brought in, not only through their R&D efforts or an outright acquisition, but through partnerships and various forms of collaboration. In short, they build an ecosystem for a future-fit business. This does not necessarily mean a change in the overall direction of their business. Many times, we find it just requires a new *how*.

We began with one organization, a financial services firm, that recognized this, and couldn't solve the challenge, using traditional business means. We were on a flight back to South Africa, and we all looked at each other and said, "I think there's a real business here. I think if we could really help solve this problem using a different model, an ecosystem-driven model, there's something real here. Should we say yes?" We said yes, and the rest is history.

When we started recognizing the potential of doing ecosystem-based work, we saw the impact that client organizations could have if they stepped beyond their organizational silos into ecosystems. Some ecosystems were built within their businesses, using cross-functional collaboration, and some extended well beyond their businesses, utilizing cross-industry collaboration and open innovation networks. I must give some credit here for like-minded organisations, who were taking a similar route to us, among them Innosight, the firm established by the late Clay Christensen, as well as Fahrenheit 212, now part of Capgemini. They asked, "What if you don't go to clients and charge by the hour? What if we have real skin in the game and jointly commit to a set of outcomes?"

With all of these experiences, and a growing client base, we decided in 2019 to write a document that would authentically share our story, how we think about the opportunities our clients face and can grow differently. It embodied our management principles and what our clients can expect from us. It became our manifesto. We make it available to anyone we work with, business partners and clients alike.

There's often a resonance, and people say, "I'd love to work with people like you." That's more important for me than any written contract or set of metrics. It's saying we're both invested, and there's something fundamental we can achieve. Let's build the ecosystem around this for a transformative outcome.

Challengers

Chris O'Byrne:

You mentioned a word that I want to dig a little deeper into—challengers. Can you tell me the definition of a challenger? What does that person look like and how do they act within a business setting?

Saar Ben-Attar:

I dedicated a whole chapter of my book to describing who challengers are and how they became our most frequent clients. A challenger can be thought about as the hero of our story, the person I'd love my readers to identify with and see themselves as.

The word "challenger" describes a mindset. We find challengers in ancient times. They were explorers who boarded ships and sailed or rode into the sunset, to discover new lands. They challenged the conventions of those days. There are challengers in the business world too, of course. They challenge how we can manage enterprises more effectively, in the new economy, founded on digital technologies and human networks. Today, we find challengers more and more of these challengers as builders of business ecosystems. I've yet to find an ecosystem, regardless of the industry—healthcare, telecommunications, media, financial services, resources, energy—where I could not identify a challenger at its essence. There's often more than one challenger in the ecosystem, as they draw other challengers in. Ecosystems are just the modern-day equivalent of past transitions, from long-held paradigms and ways industries were shaped,

to new forms. Each of these transitions needed challengers to form the bridge, between the old and the new.

Once a leader assumes a challenger mindset, a few things happen. First, they begin to see more clearly, the assumptions or paradigms under which the organization, industry, or their marketspace has been operating under. Most industry incumbents no longer see these. These assumptions become so obvious that you're bumping into them and don't even know they are there, and that's a real risk to any business.

The second step we see these leaders take is develop the curiosity to explore new business models, organizing principles, and partnerships. Using a challenger mindset equals action. They take action almost immediately after recognizing the gap, and through such action, they elicit the support and collaboration of other challengers. They even find connections within their industries to do something differently. In our sessions, they begin to draw what the new business model should look like, on a flip chart, a whiteboard, or an iPad. A new reality start taking shape in their minds. They're already in and are taking action visually, in front of us. We provide an approach for them to collaborate with others, so that they can more easily bring this new form to life.

We've run entire studies profiling challengers. We have assessment tools to measure what type of challenger you are, your unique strengths in challenging, and to what degree your mindset is helping or hindering your work.

Most importantly, we explore the practical tools you can use to have the impact you desire. This is why I get so excited about working with challengers. You see the change in front of you and how an ecosystem takes shape around them, delivering the first set of results.

Chris O'Byrne:

I have a new perspective now on what a challenger is, and it even applies to biological ecosystems. For an ecosystem to evolve, there is always a catalyst. Sometimes, it could be a change in the weather or any change. It's a change that affects the system, which then evolves. It can be positive or negative. However, when allowed to run its course in business, changes tend to lead to positive outcomes because the negative outcomes fizzle out; they don't work. A challenger is the main catalyst within a business ecosystem that leads to change. There are other outside factors, such as market changes. However, because of how quickly a business ecosystem can evolve compared to a natural one, that challenger is vital. The key position within the business ecosystem forces it to evolve positively.

Saar Ben-Attar:

Absolutely. There's always a trigger. Suppose you go to the edge of a natural ecosystem, for instance, an estuary that opens into the open sea. As the tide changes, you'll see organisms respond differently. They may find shelter, or their behavior will change as they move from the open sea into the estuary or vice versa.

The fastest rate of evolution in the natural world occurs at the edge of an ecosystem; it's the same organizing principle in business ecosystems. We must venture to the edge of our organizations, and beyond them, to build what is future fit.

Challengers purposefully place themselves at the edge of an ecosystem; that's where they find a strong sense of agency.

Regardless of industry, career, or broader aspirations, challengers purposefully place themselves at the edge of the ecosystem so they can see how the evolution might take place. They draw inspiration from nature, from social movements and interactions with other challengers, like them, for new ideas. That's an important practice we speak about in the book that makes challengers who they are—great ecosystem builders. It's because they position themselves at the edge.

It doesn't have to be for the long haul. You don't have to take yourself to the other side of the planet to do that. Some have. It's sometimes as simple as taking a walk, noticing nature, and paying attention to how different organisms communicate with one another, sitting by the seaside at sunrise, and watching the tides change. This is where the greatest epiphanies and insights happen, where challengers draw themselves into action. Then, we see them speak with their teams the next day and realize how much of an impact that encounter has had on them. They realise that they are ready to build something new.

Chris O'Byrne:

What's the biggest challenge in your work with clients, where a business-as-usual response no longer works?

Saar Ben-Attar:

That's a great question. Even the most adept of challengers have gone through periods of non-challenging and timing their response. They know when change is needed and when the business-as-usual response won't work anymore. Timing is an important practice I speak about in the book and there are ways to amplify our ability to sense the right timing to enact a challenger move.

Beyond timing, the greatest challenge is a challenger's ability to take the people around them, who are so steeped in their business as usual, into a new space—into the edge of the ecosystem—to help them see what you, as a challenger, already see. One of our clients said it nicely. He took his CEO to dinner and said, "It's going to be a very long dinner. It might be a rather liquid dinner. But I'll take one for the team because the business will look different if I can get him to see what I see." And boy, you would not believe how quickly that happened.

I have to give credit to this challenger and their CEO because both have shifted in a matter of weeks. A month later, they were sitting in front of their board and getting approval for changes we have been working with them on, to revitalize the business and partner with some of the world's largest OEMs.

You could argue the timing was right, but more than anything else, this challenger seized the opportunity to take the people closest to them to the edge of the ecosystem, so they could see what they were already seeing. That's where the biggest shifts take place, when we engage others in deep conversation, to help shift long-held perspectives.

The next big challenge becomes fighting the business-as-usual response, the anti-bodies of change, which exist in every organization. These anti-bodies want you to essentially go back to sleep; they want to numb you into believing that the ecosystem does not matter, so you won't need to be making changes. You may know in every part of your body that change is coming, that you must respond differently to how your organization behaved so far, and the business-as-usual approach won't get you there. In a leadership summit we recently held, we had a challenger CEO participate in an online simulated card game we've developed. He shared the visual that represented his mindset with several CEOs in his ecosystem. When they saw the card, they realized that they were all facing the same challenge. They all pointed to the same visuals. That was a creative way of getting others to see the challenge like them and galvanize each other into action.

There are many ways to bring others around you, even if they're steeped in the "business as usual" mindset. You might even wonder at times if it is even possible for the organization to change or if it is worth trying. My message to these challengers is that you're already more than halfway there.

You are already actively being a challenger. All you have to do now is get one or two people around you that you need in your ecosystem to venture to the edge of what they are familiar with. Some of these individuals will see their environment differently and develop clarity around the challenges they face within the organization. They'll be some of your best allies in building the ecosystem.

That probably doesn't come as a surprise for those working in the change space. However, it's particularly powerful in the age of ecosystems because the upside potential is often tremendous.

On average, across industries, once you put together an ecosystem strategy and ask the question, what is the upside potential here, the answer is three to four times of what your current strategy is able to deliver. What drives this quantum change? It's not like the underlying economic realities of your industry have suddenly changed within a mere few weeks. *It's your paradigm that has shifted. We now have the*

technologies, data, management principles, and processes to collaborate effectively in an ecosystem far better than we did when James Moore first wrote his manifesto.

Chris O'Byrne:

Can you tell me more about your Challenger CEO community?

Saar Ben-Attar:

Like many challengers do, it started as an experiment. We were throwing around ideas one day. Some of the best ideas of where to challenge and innovate came from conversations with our clients, business partners, and our broader ecosystem of experts whom we work with.

We thought, *Why don't we send some of these challengers a link to a team call, exactly like the conversation we're having now? Let's have a one-hour conversation with them. Maybe they'll prove us wrong. Maybe they'll say, no, there isn't a common process here or a method to the madness. Worst case, we would have had a good conversation and end it with that.* So, we did. We invited a dozen or so of them. I asked a good friend of mine, Chai Chuah, who serves as the Director General of Health in New Zealand, a fantastic individual, to come on as a guest and tell us about a challenging situation. He shared with us a very challenging situation, about the state of health care in the world and some of the scenarios that are playing out, how incumbent healthcare organizations were ill-equipped for these, and what could happen next.

This led to two things. First, he predicted that the prime minister of New Zealand would resign within a very short time. That happened, to our astonishment, within twenty-four hours of us recording that episode. We thought it was clearly either something he knew or managed to anticipate, using the process that we use in our work. We all had a good laugh about that one.

Second, we had a fascinating conversation with the dozen or so people in the room. Most were CEOs and other senior leaders, who could connect with the topic and bring insights from discussions held in their organizations. I closed the session and glanced at my mobile phone. It was like a Christmas tree. Everyone on that call wanted to connect with everyone else in our session. They were all messaging me, saying, "Could I connect with Chris?" "Could I connect with John?" "I want to talk to Chai." We realized we had a community in the making. We just needed a practical method to get them onto a platform. So, we did exactly that. A second session soon followed, then the third, then the fourth.

We're now celebrating almost a year to the date when we started the community, and we

have seventy-five challenger CEOs. Think of it, it began with a mere idea and a few people brainstorming some crazy ideas. That's the power of ecosystems. I wouldn't tell you it all happened in a straight line. The technology didn't always work. Once, we found out, to our horror, that the session wasn't recording the video segment, and we only had the audio. All these things happen.

However, we learned along the way. We learned about the desires of leaders as challengers, from around the world. We had people from the west coast of the United States all the way to Asia-Pacific, across continents, and time zones. We found that challengers truly wanted to sense-check their understanding of the environment around them, with fellow challengers. You could see they were coming into these sessions, not for us to give them the answers. They would come in and say, "Hey, you know what? I've got this crazy idea. We're in the middle of this challenge, crisis, or situation, and I want your view on it. What do you see?"

Those conversations got very rich very quickly. They contributed to it as much as they listened to others. That is a big part of our community. They wanted to do something together, collaborate, come to more meetings, and home in on a particular topic with fellow challengers. In some cases, they wanted to connect with

them commercially afterwards. We made sure they have the space to develop something new and innovative, in their ecosystem. Those are some of the best conversations; you suddenly recognise that you were there, in conversation zero. You were there when the idea was just a fledgling. That's the essence of a thriving community, where such connections are forged, and learning takes place laterally, across borders.

Chris O'Byrne:

As a challenger, what are you going to do differently next year? What are some of your New Year's resolutions?

Saar Ben-Attar:

Some of these are commitments in shaping. I often work with my wife on these, because once I voice them, she will be my best accountability partner. Then, I know I have to do something about them.

I've been invited to speak at a European business school at the beginning of December, which may lead to an ongoing series of lectures. At a personal level, this is quite exciting. We've also had a few inquiries from academic and research institutions, that would like to work with us in exploring new applications for ecosystem thinking, in the new year.

My second New Year's resolution is a commitment to work with two multinational firms, who are adopting the ecosystem model at scale. Our work with them is centered around the leadership aspect because that's very often the first aspect you need to tackle. You could create a wonderful strategy and have a beautifully crafted document, but it won't go anywhere without our ability to shift mindsets. We found that working with the leadership team on shifting toward an ecosystem mindset opens the door to so many other things. We've been asked, "I'm going to bring 300 leaders to our next session with you. Could you help them see that they can shift their mindset, what that feels like?" I'm very fortunate to have a wonderful team around me. We started putting things together, and within a few weeks, we had a simulated online game about how you shift mindsets. It works with up to 500 people in the virtual room. I'm excited about what we could do with them because these organizations have already committted themselves to becoming ecosystem-driven, not across the entire business necessarily, but in a particular part of the business where they see growth and have the opportunity to participate in some exciting opportunities. It's very fulfilling to help the ecosystem leadership shift. That's a big New Year's resolution.

The third thing I'm focusing on for 2024 is publishing my book, *Challengers: Harnessing the Power of Ecosystems to Collaborate and Compete in the New Economy*. That has been a journey, and I'm excited about that. It's been great to get reviews and feedback throughout the process. I've been working on this book for about eighteen months now. Then, you hand it off to editors and ask, "What do you think? Would you buy the book? What would you tell others? Would you share the news with others in your ecosystem?" We're getting some fantastic reviews, and I'm excited by that.

For anyone who's considering writing a book, I would say you need commitment, which can only come from within. Writing a book isn't something you should take lightly. However, the good news is that if you are asking me this question, you've most likely already committed. You just didn't realise it as yet. That's why people like Chris O'Byrne and others are here to help us formalize, shape, and admit to ourselves that this is part of your personal, perhaps even your spiritual development. You're bringing something new to the world. You create something that you recognize the world's needs, in some mysterious way. That's the greatest satisfaction. In January 2024, we'll be sitting on the other side of this, and the book will go live on Amazon. It's not just a book about ecosystems and the challengers that build them. Writing this book would have been impossible without the ecosystem we've built around

us. It demonstrates what an ecosystem could deliver and contribute to, in a very short time.

Chris O'Byrne:

What is the one place that people can go to learn more about you, ecosystems, and challengers?

Saar Ben-Attar:

The easiest place is my LinkedIn profile. Another is our website, ascent-growth.com. There are links to the book, our Challenger CEO community, and various public events we hold. If this resonates with you, or you've downloaded a sample chapter of the book and liked it or see the potential for this in your environment, let's have the conversation. I have committed to giving my time to these one-on-one conversations with challengers, even if you just realized you're a challenger and want to know more or connect with others, like you.

A few weeks back, I finished a conversation with a multinational company we are speaking to. A young man based in Denmark called me. He is developing this platform where ecosystem players could be remunerated for their contribution to the ecosystem. It's a form of distributed finance. It's a platform through which payments can take place autonomously, using ecosystem principles. So, you don't have to manually decide that this partner gets 30% and that partner gets 50, et cetera. You decide it upfront, and the platform distributes the value generated, in real-time, avoiding all the stops and starts along the way that payment systems generally do have. He asked if I would introduce him to this particular multinational company, because this could be tested in parallel with our work with them. A series of conversations ensued about how to optimize the ecosystem,

the role of distributed finance in it, and how to get people to want to use this solution. I have no doubt that in 2024, we will be sitting on the other side with that multinational and the myriad of partners such as him saying, "We're so glad we had that conversation." That single conversation created such resonance and helped us to connect the dots.

Whether you're a provider of technology solutions, an ecosystem orchestrator, part of a

corporate funding the ecosystem, the customer looking for the ecosystem-based services, or the nonprofit organization that wants to contribute valuable data or your time—you're a role player. Read the book. Listen to our webinar episodes. Let's talk because sometimes those brief exploratory conversations could lead us to some valuable spaces.

THE TRANSFORMATIVE POWER OF PUBLIC SPEAKING

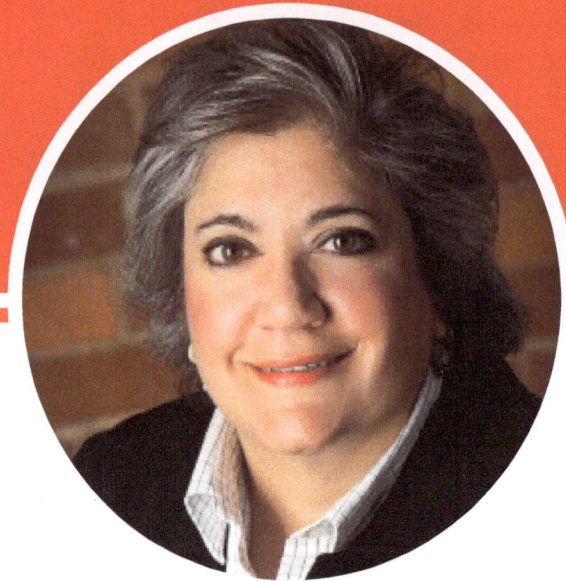

DEB SOFIELD

Chris O'Byrne

I'd like to do is start with going back to your childhood. What's a story or something that happened to you in childhood that's helped shape you into who you are today?

Deb Sofield

I'm the youngest of five, the only girl. As a speech coach, I use my outside voice inside to capture attention. Coming from a blended family with a protective atmosphere, I learned sports to be an active part of the team. My stepfather, a great guy with three sons, made sure I was well-equipped by learning to play most every sport. When I asked my brothers they wanted me to learn all those sports, they said, "We never wanted our sister to be a boring date." It's always been a humorous and adventurous journey growing up in a household where being an active participant is part of the norm.

Chris O'Byrne

How did that play out as you graduated from high school and started building your own life?

Deb Sofield

Confidence and a drive to succeed have played pivotal roles in my life, especially in sports and dealing with challenges. Despite my early foray into politics and a stint in DC, my father's wisdom led me to complete my college degree before pursuing my ambitions. I said to him, "I'm going to stay up here in DC," and he replied, "If you're not home by Thursday to finish your senior year…" I said, "Fine, I'll be home on Thursday." Having a strong foundation, including a supportive family and friends, played a vital role. As an adopted individual, I always felt like I had a golden ticket, and living up to that standard has been a source of pride endorsed by my parents.

Chris O'Byrne

So why don't you tell me what it is you do now? I know you've been doing it a long time, but what led you to that from college? What led you on this path to where you're at?

Deb Sofield

Sure. It's an interesting journey. When I expressed my desire to become a basketball coach, my parents weren't keen on financing that path. Accepting this reality, I recognized my proficiency in public speaking. I initially pursued radio and television but had a speech teacher redirect me toward public speaking, seeing my natural predisposition. Deciding to give it a shot, I found the power to sway the masses and effect change. This realization motivated me to teach these impactful skills.

Post-college, I delved into a political campaign, though we did not win. This experience taught me some life lessons I will never forget. Shifting gears, I entered the advertising agency world after being approached at a dinner party. Running an agency with a friend, I gained insight into the intricacies of printing, TV, and radio. When I sold my partnership and contemplated returning to work, requests from former colleagues prompted me to harness my skills in speech coaching and pursue my true passion of helping people express themselves succinctly.

Now, as an executive speech coach, I cater to individuals ranging from beginners to corporate presidents. My work extends to the political realm and international training for the US government overseas. Beyond coaching, I've explored sideline businesses, including hosting a radio show and publishing books. Everything I do falls under the umbrella of public speaking—whether it's interview coaching, crisis communication training, media skills training or teaching presentation skills. The common thread is helping individuals craft impactful messages, prepare for crises, and present themselves effectively to the public.

Chris O'Byrne

What do you like better, teaching or speaking?

Deb Sofield

I enjoy both, but private coaching is where my passion lies. Witnessing my clients succeed on stage brings me immense joy because I understand the hard work that goes into it. I take pride in the trust my clients place in me, guiding them to excellence. It's like extending a helping hand and saying, "Trust me, we'll shine on stage, but you need to listen and practice until it becomes second nature." A recent LinkedIn shoutout from a newer client affirmed my approach—direct, tough, but effective. In this realm, there's no room for sugarcoating.

On the stage, your reputation is paramount, and excellence is nonnegotiable. This industry is challenging, with a constant presence of individuals willing to speak for less money or claim expertise on any topic they can google. My advice: never compromise on quality. When seeking a speech coach, opt for someone with a proven track record of speaking success. If they haven't excelled as a speaker, they're unlikely to be an effective coach. It's a straightforward principle—choose wisely in this competitive arena.

Chris O'Byrne

Other than being tough, what is it that makes you unique among all the other speakers and trainers out there?

Deb Sofield

I bring a motivational approach to my coaching, coupled with a diverse background, whether in radio, television, or advertising. Starting a business, which I later sold, provided valuable insight into the intricacies of the industry. This experience ensures that printers or TV stations won't take advantage of my clients. I've learned the nuances, even in politics, where transparency is crucial—such as ensuring documentation of services, like mailing campaigns, to prevent any discrepancies.

In this business, insider knowledge is critical. With over thirty years in politics, I know the players who can be trusted and what it takes to win. Teaching at campaign schools nationwide,

I recognize the evolving challenges—public scrutiny. Demanding questions with uncertain answers. What sets me apart is my longevity and ongoing success. I don't back down, and I'm committed to constantly learning. Recently, during dinner with a client, I identified a behavior, "laughter padding," that she was aware of but didn't know how to correct. This is a simple example that illustrates my dedication to staying current and addressing evolving issues, setting me apart from those who stick to outdated methods.

It's like a dose of self-encouragement. My friends often joke that I don't need any help with my self-esteem. But here's the thing: When you've been around like you have, you know what works and what doesn't. Someone might pitch a big idea, and you're just like, "Been there, seen that." The key is trusting your instincts and knowing that your team (your team, Chris, by the way, is excellent) has got your back. I've had the pleasure of working with your team to fix some of my mishaps at KDP and other places, and trust in a reliable team is absolutely crucial. At the end of the day, trust is built, I believe, on success.

Chris O'Byrne

What are some other valuable lessons you've learned along the way?

Deb Sofield

We have to commit to keeping our word. This phrase emphasizes the importance of cutting off the bottom 10 percent. They just waste your time. It's hard, and I understand that you have to pay the mortgage.

However, they cost more than they're worth. Frankly, my price point is intentionally high, not because I don't want to help everyone—I truly do. It's akin to individuals attending campaign school without the financial means to run for office; if they can't afford the school, it raises questions about their overall readiness. In essence, it's tough love. If someone can't navigate this now, they might be occupying a seat that could be better utilized by someone with the potential to win and make a positive impact in the world.

Chris O'Byrne

Along the way, you've met all sorts of people. Who are some of those key influences or mentors that you've met along the way?

Deb Sofield

They weren't exactly mentors, but I tend to observe people's trajectories. Tony Robbins is someone I admire, though not without reservations about his vocal strain. As a speech coach, that concerns me, despite the energy from jumping around. I

appreciate the way he practices what he preaches and gives back. Contrastingly, some speakers resort to outdated methods, like selling cassettes, which can deter repeat business. Looking at the next generation, there are women with rules I don't appreciate; they lack staying power. Interestingly, I've delved into Stoic philosophy, particularly through the works of Ryan Holiday, whose insights into history inform our path forward.

It's crucial to start to recognize the timeless applicability of wisdom, even in today's fast-paced world. It's concerning that this generation is less inclined to read books, although reading on iPads is a viable alternative. As for admiration, I value success. While not a huge fan of Jeff Bezos, I've learned from his example that writing a book isn't necessarily to sell it—hello, Amazon. Another compelling lesson comes from the Netflix and Blockbuster saga. Blockbuster had the chance to buy Netflix for $50 million but deemed it too expensive. The consequence? Netflix disrupted the industry, and Blockbuster became a relic, leaving many with memories of the once-ubiquitous Blockbuster store in their towns.

I admire a lot of people, but I look for people who have disrupted something and have become successful.

Chris O'Byrne

Why do you like to teach people how to be successful?

Deb Sofield

Without sounding too hokey, I've experienced profound success, and I understand the transformative impact it can have on one's life. It's a sensation I want to share with my friends, a truly remarkable gift. I aspire to be a mentor, hoping that people will look back and attribute their present success to my influence as their coach and friend. Personally, my journey lacked numerous role models because, as a bold young person growing up with all brothers, I often felt unstoppable until life presented its own challenges.

It hasn't been a smooth ride, and I've shared with you in the past about certain environments where not being perceived as a "beautiful person" is a significant factor in determining success. I've learned to find alternative paths, discover the back door, and carve my way onto the stage in unconventional and effective ways. Some people focus on getting even with those who may have doubted them, but I believe in the power of outrageous success as the greatest form of revenge. The philosophy is simple: be so successful that they can't help but notice you.

Chris O'Byrne

What else is important to you?

Deb Sofield

We need a clear and impactful message. It's a concern when, occasionally, I come across acquaintances on LinkedIn claiming to be speech coaches without the necessary expertise. I had to address this issue because it's not just about helping a friend named "Bubba." The next person might have a real name, and if their performance on stage is compromised, it can have lasting consequences. I've encountered resistance when challenging individuals to underestimate the complexity of my profession. The ease with which some adopt consulting roles after losing their jobs is another area of concern. The prevalent willingness to work for free, for products, or for placements, especially in the age of social media, has changed the landscape significantly.

Now, why do I love what I do? It's witnessing the remarkable transformation of individuals, kind of like watching the ugly duckling become a swan. This metamorphosis is awe-inspiring, reminiscent of witnessing new birth. Whether I've played the role of a friend, mentor, or coach, the spectrum of people I've worked with is vast. I can walk into a restaurant or a parking lot and encounters with individuals who've benefited from my guidance happen frequently. These moments bring me immense satisfaction. Knowing that women have won public office after attending a campaign school where I served as the trainer fills me with pride. I derive joy from contributing to positive change in the world through the success of those I've had the privilege to mentor and coach.

Chris O'Byrne

What are your thoughts on the whole influencer phenomenon?

Deb Sofield

If you can sustain it, more power to you. In my town, there are a few influencers, good people whom I wish well. However, being an influencer isn't for everyone. What concerns me is that out of the hundreds who claim to want it, only a handful make it. The majority seem to fade away, make poor choices, and often get into trouble. I emphasize to young people the importance of choosing their friends wisely because the circle can significantly impact their choices. While breaking away is possible, navigating the world can be lonely, even in crowds. We have to help this generation find their space and shine.

Chris O'Byrne

What are your thoughts on the intersection of being a speaker and an influencer? I view the term "influencer" a bit differently than someone on YouTube doing silly stuff. It's about having genuine visibility and influence online. How does this connect with being a speaker? Do you think having a significant online presence always benefits you as a speaker?

Deb Sofield

No, and let me share something with you. It's a pattern I observed with a small group of online self-styled, self-supported folks who now lean into speaking, coaching, and being the guru of the moment. They tend to hire their friends, creating a closed circle where they interview each other. These individuals have often earned sufficient money elsewhere, enabling them to bring their friends into the fold of speaking, coaching, and being the guru of some sort.

All of a sudden, they establish a studio and start interviewing their friends. This cycle continues, with each person getting interviewed, and the pattern repeats. While this scenario is part of one of my anecdotes, I wish you success. However, I don't believe it's sustainable because, eventually, your friends fall out of favor, and consequently, you lose relevance due to a lack of substantial contributions to the benefit of others. You quantified, but you never truly imparted any knowledge after the first interview to be life changing.

One day, you decided on a one-minute rule. Fine, we all know it now. What's next? To be an influencer, you must continuously push forward. In my role as a coach and speaker, I see myself as aiding in your daily self-improvement. Each day, we progress, evolving with every stage appearance.

The most recent book I authored for you, *Perfecting Your Platform*, encapsulates everything I wish someone had shared with me as a speaker. If the room temperature is too cold, do something about it. If your audience is uncomfortable, their receptivity diminishes, a vital detail often overlooked. In your eagerness to secure payment, being overly accommodating may cause you to miss valuable opportunities.

Take a stand, be resilient—step up, man up, woman up, step up. I've transitioned from lessons I wish I had known. I documented them in a book to share because the responsibility lies with you. Years ago in Florida, I was giving a talk during a severe storm. Suddenly, a ceiling tile unexpectedly fell with a loud crash right next to me on stage. Instinctively, I thought, brain, let's go. But what if the lights came on, and the speaker had vanished?

Do you truly believe they would have thought I cared about them, that I genuinely wanted them to be successful? No. I vividly recall, as a young speaker, realizing I faced a crucial choice. I had to decide at that moment whether to be the captain of the ship, the shepherd of the flock, or simply walk out. The decision had to be made immediately.

I chose to be the shepherd of the flock. I gathered all 600 women, and we relocated to another venue to finish the presentation. Why? Because a shepherd never abandons the sheep, and the captain stands with the crew. If you possess the strength, you can find safety on the shore, or you'll leave the 99 to retrieve the one. We're all familiar with the story and its significance.

I've emphasized to speaker after speaker: If you're unwilling to do that, refrain from taking this microphone. Because within your audience, without a doubt, there's likely someone contemplating ending their life—a person so broken they turned to you for the last bit of hope. Yet, you were dismissive, uninterested, and so absorbed in your pride that your message failed to resonate. Remember it is not about you or me; it is about our message.

I deeply instill into those I train and teach that it's not about us. I learned years ago—whether you like me, Deb Sofield, or not, that's fine. I can handle criticism without harming my self-esteem; I've got enough self-esteem for myself and everyone else. It's like I pull myself out of my own perspective and place myself right next to me. Listen to this person; they can change your life. Don't concern yourself with me. I do want you to hear my message because it can help you improve in every aspect of your life. Embracing this mindset as an adult speaker completely transformed everything for me.

Chris O'Byrne

That's a good point to bring up regarding the responsibility of being a speaker because I haven't truly considered it before. However, it comes with significant responsibility. If effective speaking has the power to influence and help many people, it can also have the opposite effect. Speaking poorly or insensitively can potentially harm a lot of people.

Deb Sofield

When you assert to be a speech coach, and I'm aware that you lack expertise, merely seeking an extra $500, and knowing the potential harm if that person falters on stage, it infuriates me. If I'm aware of it, I won't hesitate to address the issue.

Chris O'Byrne

What advice do you have for people who are doing interviews?

How can I be a better interviewer even in what I'm doing today interviewing you?

Deb Sofield

First of all, I appreciate you. I genuinely think you're a fantastic person, and I have a natural affinity for you because of your consistent support. You're a skilled interviewer. I've seen interviews where the interviewer never stops talking, and the guest can't get a word in. I'm grateful that you've allowed me to tell my stories and bring you into my world.

I've encountered others in the publishing business, and your role is challenging. You have to read someone's book and decide its potential. I'm not sure if you're allowed to say when a book isn't going anywhere, but you guide us to find our way. I remember when we first met. I was in a quandary; my publisher vanished, and you came to my aid. You listened when I was at the end of my rope, having invested a lot in getting my first book out. Your kindness and support, especially during that challenging time, define your approach. Our friendship has endured, and your modus operandi is to assist people in getting their books to market. The rest is up to us to keep moving forward.

Chris O'Byrne

It's thanks to people like you that make it possible. And this is the bragging point. We've handled over 15,000 books— it's been quite a journey. The responsibility hits home when I think about how many people I affect through what I do. It's not just about the authors; it extends to everyone touched by those books. Each book becomes a platform, influencing readers and those connected to them. That perspective has shaped my approach. You mentioned off-camera about speaking as a spiritual business. Can you elaborate on that?

Deb Sofield

During our brief conversation, I noticed that many speakers nowadays tend to delve into that avenue, as I believe most people are in search of something.

As a speaker, I hope it's true that you don't want to be dishonest in your faith. However, what I've observed in this business is that if you're a truly effective speaker, you can be life changing. You can help someone in drawing a line in the sand and declaring, "Today is the day."

I've encountered speakers who love their audience, and that's the key difference. I realize this may sound unusual, but for me, it's not. When I attend a conference, I make my way to the room where I'm scheduled to speak. I sit quietly, saying a prayer over the room because that's who I am. No one needs to know I do that. Occasionally, the camera crew inquires, "What are you doing in here?" and I respond, "I'm just getting a feel for the room." I believe a good speaker will engage in a practice like this.

I am also a clergy coach. If you're a pastor or a preacher embodying a steadfast commitment to Jesus, and your message remains confined to the stage, what good does it serve? It's akin to salt losing its saltiness—the very essence of loss, rendering is no more than something to discard.

The issue is hearing speakers who seem to be captivated by the stage, only to disappear after. I reflect on this, realizing that within their purview are 8,000 people, and among them, there are people for whom they might be the last hope. So, it's not solely about the speaker; it's about the message. I firmly believe that messages should inspire hope. I often recount the story of Rudy Giuliani after 9/11; he faced the cameras and declared, "We will rebuild. "We're going to come out of this stronger than before -- politically stronger, economically stronger"

I compare this with Kathleen Blanco, the former governor of Louisiana. When asked for her thoughts after Hurricane Katrina, she looked at the camera and said, "It's hopeless." True leaders lead people to hope, and I believe, as a speaker, that's an integral part of our role.

Despite being a trainer, my focus also lies in crisis communication. I emphasize this because, in situations where someone is injured, there's uncertainty in the building, or a fire has broken out, it's imperative not to send someone unprepared and lacking composure. While I grasp the business aspect, it's crucial to recognize that these situations involve people's lives.

I believe the more effective speakers are those who understand that the message, and the words have to come together. It's not a universal skill; I get that. If you're immersed in reading a budget report, I understand. However, with that budget report, I urge you to elevate it to the next level. I acknowledge it may sound a little silly, but behind those numbers in the budget report are the financial resources supporting people's families. There's more significance here, and you need to find the joy in that.

I work daily with young people pursuing medical school, dental college, and law careers. In my role as an interview coach, I encounter many with a stellar 4.0 GPA. That's impressive, but what sets you apart? Have you built a habitat house or gone on a mission trip? It's about more than

academic achievements. What have you done? When parents ask how to guide their child, I advise creating a diverse mosaic of experiences. People crave connection, and as a speaker and coach, entering a room and offering a prayer is my way of establishing that connection. It's a responsibility I take seriously, recognizing the value of their time.

I believe this sentiment resonates among many of your accomplished speakers—both the good and the exceptional ones. The $500 speaker may not share the same level of commitment, or perhaps they do, but it's not their daily focus. In this industry, longevity establishes a pattern;

you understand your needs and your body's requirements. There's a set of rules for success: prioritize a good night's rest and avoid excessive socializing. These insights are crucial, and I've included them in my latest book because if someone doesn't share this wisdom, how are you supposed to know?

Chris O'Byrne

Absolutely, that's the challenge. We often assume people know what to do. Now, in a more practical context, while I don't engage in a lot of public speaking, I do conduct various interviews and discussions. However, I have an upcoming talk in a group setting, and it's been about three

months since my last major stage appearance. I have around an hour and a half for this talk. What suggestions, tips, and techniques do you recommend for me?

Deb Sofield

I haven't seen your speech yet, but I would undoubtedly suggest you make your ending the beginning. Build to wow. What does that mean to build to wow? When we were in English class, you had to build your paper or speech to a denouement. You don't do that anymore. This is a TikTok generation. What do you have to say to me? And then you back it down. The problem is that everybody wants to build to wow, and the audience has already moved on.

One crucial lesson from radio is the proximity to the next station, merely a centimeter away. Without an engaging start, the audience is lost. It's imperative not to be mundane. For instance, never open with a generic greeting like, "Well, good morning," if you are the third speaker of the day." The audience has heard that before, and they'll tune out. Instead, step onto the stage and ask, "Do you know in America today?... then pause and give your fact or figure to capture your audience attention immediately" Incorporate facts and figures—make them meaningful. However, a story is indispensable. It must be your story, authentic and relatable.

Nobody desires a lengthy speech. Most people react negatively to extended speeches; they don't want that.

Start late, end early— who minds if you end early? Nobody. Who minds if you go over? Most people, especially if you're the last meeting of the day. If it's between you and beer, you're done.

As for speakers, here's the deal: If you're the morning speaker, lean a little more educational—facts, figures, stories. If you're the afternoon speaker, shift toward entertaining stories with fun information. Evening speakers, no facts—we want stories. Think about it. When we come home after work, we click on the TV for entertainment. If you're going to deliver a raw campaign speech, sorry, I'm done. I'm not listening. I'll find something to do.

Consider the time of day, audience temperature, and venue—where are you? All those things have to be taken into consideration. You decide if you want to be a rock-star speaker, or if you want to be average, then do what you've always done. But I would say start with the end in mind. Stephen Covey was right. You've got to know. Your audience wants to know. And your audience wants to know how long you're going to speak.

But nine times out of ten, when working with the president of a

corporation, I make the ending the beginning, the great story.

I received a call from a client. Actually, the wife called and said, "My husband's the president of a corporation. The company stock is in the tank. We've had a terrible situation. Everyone's mad at him. What are we going to do?" I responded, "Okay, I'll be happy to come." When I arrived, I had to meet him at the house, and his wife had to be there because he didn't want anyone interfering with the speech. He emphasized, "Coach, I'm the president of the corporation."

Upon entering, I said, "All right, let's talk about the stock then." The response was, "No, we can't talk about the stock." I said, "You have to talk about the stock. This whole audience wants to hang you." We arranged it in a way for him to share the true story of what happened. The product got stuck off a ship in California, and due to union issues, it didn't make it to port. Consequently, they missed the Christmas season. Missing the holiday season is quite a setback, but it happened. Nothing worked, and everyone was upset. He was the new president, so he was to take the fall.

I proposed, "What we're going to do is walk onto the stage but not to the seat of power, (the lectern). We'll go halfway, you will stop, and we'll spotlight you, and you'll say, 'Before I begin, let me tell you what happened to the stock.'" We shared the story. Then, when he was finished explaining what happened, he moved to the lectern (the seat of power), and he gave the rest of his company report. When he finished, it resulted in the longest applause ever, with not a single question from the audience.

They called me to thank me as they were leaving for a weekend getaway. He was so relieved, and she, too, felt a sense of relief because she understood how much it weighed on him.

But what do most people say? "Well, let's just hide." You can't. You've got 800 people who want to know what happened to the stock. And you know what? We laid it out. This happened. We made a mistake. We're never going to this port again. We're going to make a change for next time. Hang with us. We're doing the best we can. Remember, you really do not want your audience asking questions. If you are not careful, questions can start a fight.

If I hear you as a speaker, Chris, and you get a question from the audience, I will incorporate the answer to that question into your next talk. You never should get the same question twice. It reflects laziness. Even if you have to say, "You know, people often ask me," answer the question. Always answer the question.

Because if you get an audience member who suddenly gets the spotlight effect, thinking they're going to take you down, they'll try to bring you down, and the audience becomes meaner and angrier than I've ever seen before. My job is to protect my speakers, and I do that by answering that question if it has come up before. That's one less thing you have to worry about.

Chris O'Byrne

So, if I start with the end in mind—or if I start with the end—what do I end with?

Deb Sofield

You're likely going to wrap it back up again, with a recap of what we discussed. But again, I've likely cut your speech in half by now since we started at the end. This allows time for Q&A that are new or a positive response to your presentation. Remember, as a speaker, you're doubly assessed by your ability to answer questions, so you better be ready.

Chris O'Byrne

What about humor?

Deb Sofield

That's tough. I'd suggest finding a quote, maybe something from Reader's Digest. But be careful. My rule is, if it's not funny, don't use it. Why? Everyone is waiting to be offended. Rule number

10 (of my 15 Rules for the Road presentation) is everyone's waiting to be offended. It might be fun with your friends on Friday night at the bowling alley. But is not on Monday morning. They'll forgive you, but they won't forget. And you didn't mean to do it. I don't know anybody who wakes up and says, "Today is the day I'm going to offend them." But because I said something stupid or silly that I thought was funny, I hurt their feelings, and I never meant to do that. It's hard. You've got to be careful.

I maintain an Excel spreadsheet with 1,683 quotes, cutting and pasting each one I come across. As a speaker, it's an honor to be invited back, and when stated, "We had you last year," I respond with, "What do you want me to do this year?"

Given this, I always aim to present fresh information. However, it's crucial to include a few quotes that resonate with you. Not only do quotes showcase your intelligence and extensive reading, but they also help the audience connect with you. In my public speaking classes, designed for those less inclined to listen, I often inquire, "Who's learned a new word?" The response is typically minimal, highlighting the importance of continuous learning.

New word alert! During Joe Kennedy's presidential campaign, he introduced

"Malinformation," signifying information the government conceals but acknowledged as true. Witnessing the birth of such terms is intriguing. I recently stumbled upon another gem on my computer; I've labeled it "New Words." Today's word is "Spuddle," a 17th-century term meaning to work ineffectively, appearing busy while achieving nothing. It's synonymous with muddling. What's your latest vocabulary addition?

Being one step ahead of your audience is vital. It necessitates a continuous learning process. About that laughter padding: I've never encountered it before, but now that I have, I've noticed it in a few of my clients. Always be learning.

Chris O'Byrne

That's good advice for me because I'm one of those people who always thinks I'm funny until my wife tells me otherwise. Slowly, I've learned to keep my mouth shut when I think I'm going to be funny. It doesn't work every time, but it's greatly improved.

Deb Sofield

Here's the good news. The more you do it, the better you become. I was the emcee for an event, ; and the audience members were supposed to speak for a minute. Well, of course, they're politicians, so they wanted to talk and talk, and I said, "Hey, guys, a

New York minute, not a Southern minute." The audience broke out in laughter because Southern minutes go much longer than a New York minute. Let's get it done, people. I had to break the ice so that I didn't offend the speakers, but I had to let him know we've got to keep moving here because I have seven speakers to go.

Chris O'Byrne

What are some parting words of wisdom to leave us with?

Deb Sofield

Cherish your audience. Discover a genuine reason to love them. When you genuinely care about your audience, both you and they are elevated. It's palpable; they sense it, they recognize it. If this connection starts to fray for you, it might be time to step back. Your performance may be losing its edge. Seek out a new audience or assist younger people in finding theirs. I understand it's essential to evolve and stay connected.

As I age, I find myself pondering when someone will inevitably ask, "When is she going to exit the stage?" After all, there's an abundance of opportunities out there. If I choose never to step away from the limelight or stay in it, I've contemplated this notion, especially observing certain individuals at speaking conferences. The question arises:

When will they graciously bow out? Their narrative has lost its comedic charm.

There's was a gentleman who was once pretty overweight but has shed a considerable amount. Surprisingly, he continues to share the same outdated fat jokes. The audience is left puzzled—he's no longer heavy, and new spectators wouldn't even know he used to weigh 500 pounds. While his transformation is indeed an incredible life story, it's not the narrative he needs to keep delivering. Persisting with these fat jokes hurts his messaging. It appears it might be time for him to gracefully exit the stage.

So, I believe that's one aspect. Additionally, I would emphasize that this generation requires our support more than ever, both as friends and mentors. But I also want you to explore fresh terminology. Recently, I was on a plane and came across an article on brutalist architecture. Unfamiliar with the term, I discovered that my hometown's Museum of Art follows this style—characterized by its Soviet design style, featuring concrete walls. It's aptly named brutalist architecture. So, expand your vocabulary. It's fascinating how we consider ourselves intelligent until we encounter individuals with truly profound knowledge and a great vocabulary.

Then it dawns on you that there's more to learn. It's time to step away from Facebook and dive into a good book or, perhaps, understand the current state of the world. My advice is simple: Do your job. Do your homework, and be the very best. Despite any self-importance, remember, kindness matters. I leave you with a quote from Mark Twain that resonates with me: "Kindness is a language that the deaf can hear and the blind can see." In a world that needs kindness, these words hold true.

Action Steps

1. **Embrace your unique background**: Leverage your personal experiences and diverse background to add depth and authenticity to your business approach. The author's journey highlights how varied life experiences, from family dynamics to professional shifts, can enrich your perspective and decision-making in business.

2. **Develop effective communication skills**: Focus on honing your public speaking and presentation abilities. The author's transition from politics to speech coaching underscores the power of persuasive communication in business, whether in client interactions, team leadership, or public presentations.

3. **Adopt a continuous learning mindset**: Stay open to learning and adapting, just as the author did throughout their career. This approach keeps your business strategies fresh and relevant, enabling you to navigate the evolving challenges and opportunities in your industry effectively.

About the Author

Deb Sofield is a keynote speaker, author of five books, *Speak without Fear – Rock Star Presentation Skills to get People to Hear What You Say*, and her new book *Perfecting Your Platform ~ Transforming Your Stage Presence into Stage Power*, her book series *Encouragement for Your Life ~ Tough Love Memos to Help You Fight Your Battles and Change the World*, volumes 1-3. Deb is a radio talk show host in the Salem Network, podcaster and president of her own Executive Speech Coaching Co., which trains people for success in speaking, crisis communications, presentation skills, media, and message development.

To learn more about Deb, visit http://www.debsofield.com

To purchase her books, visit https://amzn.to/34Wab0n

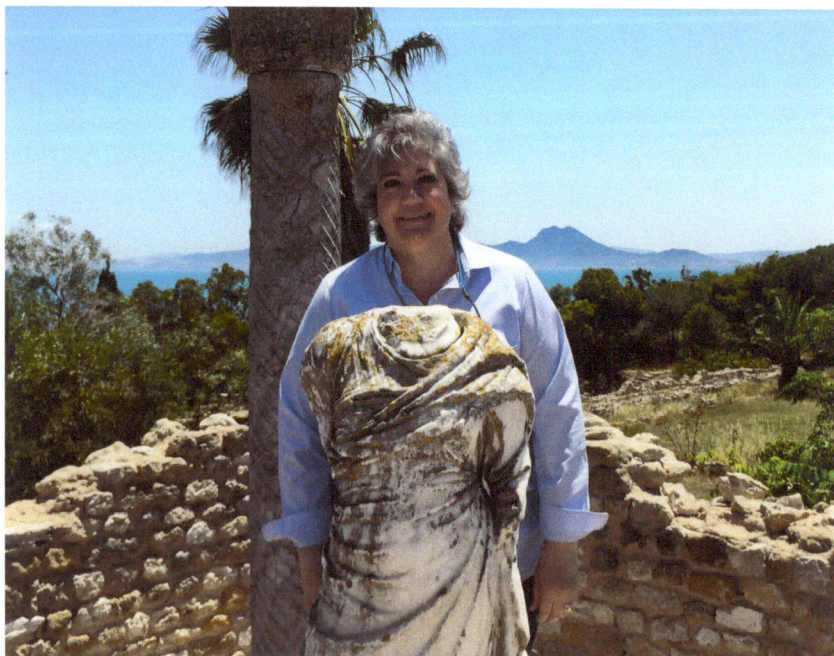

RSS RELIABLE
STAFF SOLUTIONS
www.ReliableStaffSolutions.com

DOING GOOD IS
GOOD BUSINESS

SHARING THE CREDIT

Your business can give to charity without writing a check. Visit **www.SharingTheCredit.com** and start giving today.

DRIVING THE FUTURE OF E-LEARNING WITH MICROCASTING

KEN BURKE

Chris O'Byrne

Ken, share with us the story of what led you to your current work.

Ken Burke

I started my entrepreneurial journey very young. Right out of MBA school, I started a company called MarketLive. That wasn't the original name, but it turned into MarketLive. I ran that company for twenty-one years. It gave me the energy to create companies. I raised quite a lot of money from the Silicon Valley. Sequoia Capital was my first investor. They are one of the most prominent and well-known VC firms in the world. However, I didn't raise money until about thirteen years into the business. I just funded it through the School of Hard Knocks, if you will, learning entrepreneurship for the first thirteen years of the business.

We ended up with hundreds of customers. It was an ecommerce

platform company. We became one of the world's largest and most successful ecommerce platform companies, ranked in the top five of Gartner and Forrester, which ranks enterprise platforms worldwide. We did over two billion dollars a year in online commerce for our customers (like Armani and Party City).

We had so many customers—Johnson & Johnson, Disney, Warner Bros. Now, they're all returning to me. It was a fantastic learning ground for entrepreneurship, and I loved it. I ended up selling the company about six years ago, then took a year off and traveled the world, which was phenomenal. Like many people reading this right now, I'm an entrepreneur, and I couldn't stay away. I just wanted to get back into it. I wanted to have purpose and drive and create something. I always say that with the entrepreneurial brain that created a company, you can't just turn it off when you sell the company. It doesn't leave you. That brain keeps going, that sixteen hours a day of *What am I doing? How am I creating? What am I building?*

I love growing things. So, I jumped in, but I didn't want to do e-commerce again. I could go back into it, but I had done it for twenty-one years and was bored. Even though e-commerce is still a great area, and I could have built another business (or two or three) around it, I wanted to jump into e-learning. I don't know why; it was just a desire of mine.

I started by saying, "I've got to learn how to do this." Then, I created EntrepreneurNOW, which educates entrepreneurs worldwide on how to write business plans, develop strategies, become an entrepreneur, and develop an entrepreneurial mindset. My curriculum is used all around the world at prestigious universities and throughout a bunch of different learning environments. However, what I wanted to do was to learn how to create the content. So, I hired a big production crew and spent too much money on my content creation. Don't do the same thing I did because you don't have to spend much money. I had a Hollywood film crew. I had multicamera shots. I had lights, camera, action—everything. I learned how to build content from the ground up and build excellent content. I got good at it. Then, I began distributing it and receiving royalties from LinkedIn Learning and all these different learning sites. I thought, *What do I do next?*

I'm a software guy who always wanted to build another software platform. So, my CTO and I built a platform called Microcasting. I was the visionary for it. We have many customers and build e-learning environments for customers we love. Whether they want to use e-learning for sales and marketing purposes, thought leadership purposes, or to sell their content, they want to sell. They want to do ecommerce. My

background is in ecommerce, so I built ecommerce into the engine. Our platform is feature rich and does anything you want to do to integrate e-learning into your business; it does customer portals, ecommerce, whatever you need. We won't go into the details of that right now, but I have to tell you that the genesis for starting is that I love to grow things, cultivate businesses, and add value. That's what supercharges me every day.

Chris O'Byrne

There are other many other e-learning platforms. What makes Microcasting so unique and special?

Ken Burke

There are many e-learning platforms—many old and tired ones, in my opinion. There are plenty in traditional corporate America. We created a new approach to e-learning, integrating AI and combining other things, such as a sales and marketing system attached to a CRM system, as much as anything else. We look at e-learning from how the user experiences the content. How do we integrate it with what you're doing offline? We call it a hybrid model where you might coach or share your thought leadership or knowledge with the world. How do you leverage e-learning as part of a component of that? We're an e-learning business system but have other unique features. I could get into the details, but basically, it's what we would call a multi-portal system, which allows you to have one e-learning site. Still, many versions of your e-learning site are instantly created so that the user experience can be customized and personalized for that individual user or individual group you might be selling to. That's highly unique in our industry.

We look at it through a different lens. I wanted to create as much an e-learning platform as a thought leadership platform for people. People must establish themselves as thought leaders in today's world. There's no question about it. I did that in my e-commerce company, and that's how I grew it from zero to selling it for a lot of money. We did that for one reason: I was a thought leader in the e-commerce industry for twenty-one years, bringing in significant customers, which I mentioned earlier, and we're doing the same thing. However, now, I'm creating a platform that others can use to become thought leaders. That's one of the most significant uses of our platform, in addition to selling your content and programs.

Chris O'Byrne

What are some of the more unusual uses you've seen people using Microcasting for?

Ken Burke

I was surprised at how many people we have in the medical industry. That wasn't an industry we were going after at first, but there's a whole world in the medical and financial industries. But what have we designed it for? It's not necessarily surprising, but I'm thrilled to see people using it as a sales and marketing tool to collect leads and nurture their customers. If you're selling to a customer—and all of you out there are selling to somebody— you must nurture them. As you're doing that, you're building a relationship. It warms my heart to see people sending out their e-learning free of charge to their prospects. Why is it free of charge? Because sending out bits and pieces of their e-learning is specifically designed to help that customer convert. So, my customers are sending it out to their end users to help them along the sales cycle. Maybe you have a one-month or a three-month sales cycle. You're building trust, authority, and thought leadership. As you build that relationship with the customer, they're much more likely to convert when you're working with them and bringing them along. That's one of the significant use cases that we have out there. Every time I see it, I get excited about it.

Chris O'Byrne

There's so much possibility and opportunity in that. Even though you and I have talked several times, I'm still trying to wrap my head around all the opportunities there. For example, I tell people you must have one place to send people. If I get on a podcast somewhere, I want to send them to one place. How does yours work as a lead gen tool?

Ken Burke

This can be broader, where you can explain your offline or additional coaching services depending on the individual coach, consultant, small business, or whoever is using the platform. We've built a lot of technology in our software, so when somebody comes into the site, we have a marketing-oriented version of the site. You don't have to sell them something, but you can collect leads, give away free content, or open it to the public so they can instantly access content; they don't even need to register. They don't need to do anything.

When they register for a free membership, enroll in a course (because you can have an enroll button as well), or sign up for a paid membership, the site instantly converts over to their fulfillment site. It's the same site and the same URL; everything is all the same. It's transparent to the user. They have marketing experience where they can market anything. It doesn't have to be e-learning; you can market your traditional business. Then, as they transition from a nonmember to a member, we can reconfigure the site into a free membership site, an enrolled site, or a full-on paid membership, and the sites will configure accordingly, all under the same banner. One website, not ten.

Chris O'Byrne

What's another one of your favorite features of Microcasting?

Ken Burke

I love so many things about Microcasting, but I have to tell you about one of our inventions. I don't know if it was our invention, but we created it. It's called the learning board, which allows you to customize the individual learning experience. So, if I'm the professor, coach, consultant, or whatever, I can drag courses onto their palette or learning board. We call them Microcasts, which are videos, courses, or programs. I just drag them on, and they're automatically alerted that they have something on their learning board. The learning board can show up in the universal nav as a dominant area, and it shows up in the My Learning section. It's a communication vehicle where they're communicating one-on-one. You're crafting that learning experience for an individual, which I love. But we made it easier.

We've put in some additional things so you can drag and drop whole groups of things in. It makes it a lot easier so that you don't have to do all the work. We're adding a bunch of AI into the engine as well, and I have to say I love the integration of AI and e-learning. You can do so much, such as creating video summaries. When you upload a video or a course, the AI engine takes the transcript, which we automatically generate out of our engine. Everybody gets that now. Then we move that over automatically into ChatGPT and say, *Summarize this* or *Develop five bullet points*, or *Develop critical points for this video*. Then, that shows a supportive text below the video as an example, one of many examples of auto-writing learning objectives, quizzes, and descriptions. We're doing all of that in our labs and will be releasing that very soon. I'm excited about that. I'm excited about the auto-creation of courses.

Now, I want to be very careful here. I don't necessarily want AI to be the spokesperson for your course, but I want to help you use AI as a tool to create the outline. In our engine, you approve each piece of the outline, then move over to where you create the script and graphics that might accompany it. Ultimately, you're using AI step by step, approving each course section.

I recommend you film the course itself so you can have all the creative control of the course. I want it to be *your* course. I don't want it to be an AI course that you can generate in five minutes. By the way, go into ChatGPT and try to generate a course. It won't turn out very well. If you do it using my method, you're thinking about each lesson, so you create the outline, which creates the lessons and gives you all the ideas for the lessons. You think about it: *Is that all that I want? Do I want to add more?* Next, take those lessons and tell ChatGPT to create each lesson and how long you want the lesson to be. After review, that can be dumped into our engine as well. But I still want you to record it.

We have technology that will simulate all of that, but I think the authenticity of making a human connection is essential. If you want to go the cheap route, there are technologies out there that will also do the video for you.

We're just beginning with all of this, too. This is the first year the rest of the world can touch AI. We used to call it personalization for twenty-five years. That is what MarketLive did. Our team at Microcasting is nearly the same team as MarketLive. We've been doing this for many years, but this is the first year that actual humans and the business world have been able to touch AI. We're just getting started. So much will happen in the next five to ten years, but it's been around for a long time. This isn't a new concept. It's just an evolution where ordinary businesspeople can interact with it and quickly obtain outstanding results. And that's great. I use ChatGPT all the time. I love it.

Chris O'Byrne

How much does somebody need to put into the production of their course to make it effective?

Ken Burke

Learn from my mistakes. You don't even want to know how much I needlessly spent on production. My first program had twenty-five individual courses, each one about thirty to forty-five minutes. The entire program was about twenty hours long. I even had worksheets. It's the course of all courses. If you want to run a business, that is a great course. It probably cost me $150,000 to develop. What a mistake. Now, I sit right in the studio with a green screen in the back. I have my two lights here, my camera, and my teleprompter. I can build a course in my studio that costs me under $1,000.

Our website has a course called Building Your Studio for Under $1,000. It's even possible to do it for under $500. You can build the studio with everything you need. I can record a course in an hour and usually don't have to rerecord it. It takes a couple of hours to build the PowerPoint. If I know quite a bit about it, the time spent is minimal. Then, I come

into my studio and turn on the camera. That's all you need.

I way overspent back in the day. Now, my courses are even better. Maybe five hours at most is spent on doing them, and that's it. Also, I do all my editing within those five hours. If you want to hire someone else to work on it, look at platforms like Fiverr, where you pay a fee for services rendered. There's not a lot of money involved in this. I want people building courses to be thinking. I want them to be the experts. I want them to deliver the content engagingly. One of the tips I teach is to look at the camera and notice I'm making eye contact with it.

I want you to get that monitor right in front of you. I recommend using a relatively inexpensive Logitech Brio webcam. I use my Rode mic for about the same price. It's the best in the industry. Spend money on your mic. It's a reasonable investment. Also, I love that I can just pop this into my suitcase because I travel a lot, and in case I ever need to do a podcast, it doesn't take up much room. It's the best investment you'll make—and maybe the most expensive—but your mic is everything. You want it to work flawlessly.

By the way, consider recording at 720p if your computer can't keep up with 1080p. If it keeps up with 1080p, you're fine. When you upload your videos to our

system (or any system), we will shrink those files so they can be delivered to the end user via the web. So, everybody records it in super high quality and creates these ginormous files. When I process all of them, I shrink them down. The quality is still there. You would never tell the difference. Most professionals would say that you want to record at 1080p in Hollywood. What you don't want in your video is lag time. Accordingly, we don't want to jerk, hesitate, or when you can't hear my words. Sometimes, when your computer can't keep up with recording at 1080p, I record lower sometimes. That's good to keep in mind.

Chris O'Byrne

I do a lot of interviews. Can I turn my interviews into a course?

Ken Burke

That's my favorite topic in the world! I do it at least once a week now. I've got onc to borrow on podcasting with a podcast expert. I'm so excited about this because I love the idea of podcasting. I do these interview courses every week because they're so fast. Let me give you the secret to it.

I call it the interview method. I'd like to say I created the method, but I'm not that arrogant, so I won't say that. But I didn't steal it from anybody. I just made it up and started using it. I've done somewhere around a hundred of these. In many ways, they're better than doing courses on my own. Right now, Chris and I are having an engaging discussion. We're both really into it. The people watching us are also into it because we're going back and forth. It's not just me droning on about creating the perfect course, but I've created a course called the interview method and am happy to give it away for free. It's a thirty-minute course on how to do this method. But let me give you a couple of tips on it.

Number one, do a pre-interview call. That's key because we have to break up our interview into lessons. So, as Chris is asking me questions, he is probably thinking in the back of his mind, *How can I break this video up? I don't want to run it for thirty or forty minutes. I don't want to make it a webinar. I'm asking very structured questions. I'm not letting Ken go off and talk about crazy stuff. I'm keeping him on target.* That's exactly what Chris is doing right now. He's interviewing me, using the interview method, and can take this video we're doing right now on StreamYard, a tool we both use. (I love it, especially for only twenty bucks a month!) You're good to go.

It does everything you need. It's like CNN in a box. Essentially, I will chop this into seven or eight lessons (or Chris will), or I'll do this tomorrow with my podcasting. The key to the whole thing is a structured interview. Do not let people go off on tangents. We have to keep them focused. If you do the pre-interview call, you get a compelling title. (I teach you how to write a compelling title.) Then, we structure five steps to a better life, or ten steps to this, etc. It doesn't have to be steps. It can be figurative buckets for whatever the topics are.

The buckets are made to be two to five minutes of answering. Of course, I talk a lot, so Chris probably structured it accordingly, but two to five minutes, seven minutes maximum, into each little bucket. Before you know it, we have an introduction and conclusion, a structured course. Then, I add a quiz to it, which I write using ChatGPT. I write my lesson descriptions after I get a transcript, and I've got my course. That's how you do it. I just gave you the whole course in about two minutes.

Chris O'Byrne

What is something that you want to leave people with to understand more about Microcasting or creating courses?

Ken Burke

The most important thing is through Microcasting, we're trying to be your partner in your e-learning endeavor. We provide a lot of education, services, and other things. We don't charge for any of it. It's our business model. You might learn from our business model as well. We provide all the services that we do free of charge, and we do that for a reason: We want you to utilize the software and do so in the best way you possibly can. I want you to be coached on building engaging courses that will get consumed. I don't want you to build long courses that nobody ever watches that are not attractive and engaging. That's one of the things we work on. We have all the plumbing and everything, but the whole ball of wax is the business model.

Will you use a hybrid model? Will you be on demand? Will you be live? Will you be membership-based? Will you be commerce-based? Thinking about all of that and how it all comes together is what we help people with. Again, it's free of charge. It's part of our knowledge about how we see our customers working and what model makes the most sense. What model makes the most sense for you? If you use the hybrid model, it is straightforward: *How much of my time will they get one-on-one? How much of my time will they be in the group? How much on-demand will they get?* On a scale of 1–100, we determine where that works and the balance that is right for your business. Next, we'll teach you how to associate a premium or value-based price. I have a module on how to do value-based pricing, where you learn to get the real value out of your delivery.

That's the key, the part I love. It's not just the mechanics of e-learning. It's *everything*. That's what our company stands for and what we're all about. We love doing it every day. I've been doing it all day. I haven't been on the phone all day. This is fun.

Chris O'Byrne

What is the one place that you would like people to go to learn more about you?

Ken Burke

We have a site called Microcasting.com that you can go to and learn more about our platform, me, and our different programs. We also have a little learning center with free content that teaches you how to do e-learning well, how to use the interview method, how to create the perfect course, how to set up your studio, and a lot more at learningcenter.microcasting.com.

About the Author

Ken Burke, founder and CEO of The EntrepreneurNOW! Network, is a speaker, serial entrepreneur, mentor, and author. Ken founded MarketLive, a software platform generating $2 billioin in online sales through the platform. He sold MarketLive to Vista Equity Partners in 2016. Ken has taught well over 10,000 entrepreneurs how to successfully start and grow their companies. His courses are viewed by students all over the world. Ken recently published his book, *Prosper: 5 Steps to Thriving in Business and Life*. His alma mater, the University of Southern California–Marshall School of Business, later awarded him the honor of Entrepreneur of the Year.

MICROCASTING

Supercharge Your Business!

Do you want to find new ways to add additional income to your coaching, consulting, or content creation business?

eLearning Portals by Microcasting is specifically designed for Coaches, Consultants, and Course Creators to engage your customers, establish yourself as a thought leader, and grow your revenues.

Here are just a few things you can do with **Microcasting**:

- ⊘ **Start selling** your courses and programs.
- ⊘ Create a **paid membership site** to grow your revenues.
- ⊘ Build a free membership site to **increase lead gen**.
- ⊘ Easily **integrate eLearning** into your marketing website.
- ⊘ Create **individualized customer portals** .
- ⊘ And so much more...

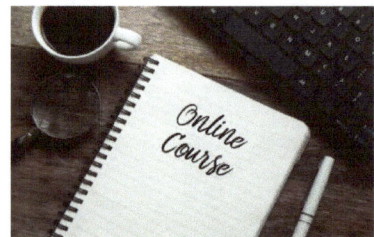

Microcasting is an all-in-one online learning platform that makes it easy for course creators to design, manage, and market their courses. With its personalized eLearning experience, you can keep your current customers engaged with your business, generating more upsells and higher renewal rates. Create courses quickly and effortlessly - all with the help of Microcasting!

Try Microcasting today and start transforming your business!

USING INTERROGATION TECHNIQUES FOR BUSINESS GROWTH

DANIEL HAMMOND

Chris O'Byrne:

Daniel, can you give me a brief overview of what you do?

Daniel Hammond:

I have a practice called Business Interrogation. I interview entrepreneurs and ask them about their biggest business challenge. It's a twenty-minute session. It's timed. I have a checklist of things I go through, and it's focused on helping the business owner get clarity around whatever their challenge is. Then we brainstorm some solutions as well. Sometimes, that's solving a problem, untangling an issue, or maximizing something new they're doing that they've never done before.

Chris O'Byrne:

That is a very concise explanation because I know there's a whole lot more to it, but I love the story that led up to it. What did you do after graduating high school?

Daniel Hammond:

There was a chance that I wasn't going to graduate high school. I ended up getting challenged by school. I'm a fast learner but not a good student in traditional schooling. That's always been a challenge for me, especially rote memorization. Biology and languages have always challenged me. I work well under pressure and managed to cram for two years of Latin in three days. I went from being the worst out of sixty students to having the third-highest comprehensive final exam, and fortunately for me, a high enough score to pass the class and graduate.

Once I graduated high school, I tried college for a year and a half. It was an extension of the challenges I already faced in school. Then I started working, and I loved working. I started as an assistant manager at a convenience store when I was eighteen. I often ran into the challenge of getting to a place where I had no more growth, and in this case, I was doing so much work for my manager that my manager wasn't recommending that I have my own store because she liked that I was doing all her work. Eventually, I found another opportunity as an assistant manager trainee at Little Caesars Pizza. I moved

from assistant manager trainee to assistant manager in two weeks to co-manager in two months. By the fourth month, I was a unit manager. By month ten, I was a training manager. Stuck again because I did not see a reasonably short path to promotion for a 22-year-old to district supervisor.

Eventually, I joined the US Army. At twenty-three, I was a bit older going than most going into the army. I maxed out the entry test and qualified for any job in the Army. I asked what the hardest thing to qualify for was. They said it was a signals intelligence collector. I looked at my options, and enlisted with Airborne with Spanish guaranteed in my contract. Spanish wasn't easy, but I eventually learned basic Spanish and jumped out of airplanes without hurting myself too badly.

Chris O'Byrne:

What about that led you to where you are now?

Daniel Hammond:

I learned a lot of lessons in the Army. I did four years of active duty, a year and a half of school, and two and a half years in the 82nd Airborne Division. When I got out, I went into the US Army Reserves and switched over to interrogation. I enjoyed the course and I guess I was so unnaturally good at it that they handed me a diploma and said,

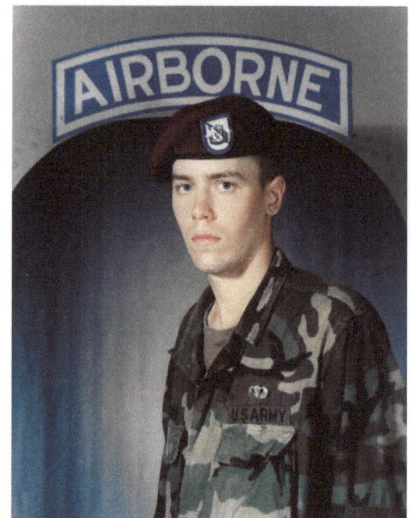

"Transfer to our unit. You need to be teaching this stuff."

I taught interrogation for six years in the reserves and had a deployment. That gave me real-world interrogation experience. I like connecting with people and finding win-win situations. Even in real-world interrogations where you're talking to people you would think would not want to help you, I am good at finding common ground with people and was a successful interrogator. In interrogation and in general, I build and maintain excellent rapport with people.

My boss was amazed one day when we walked into the prison camp, and one of the prisoners started waving to me. I waved back, and my boss asked, "Who's that?" I responded, "I have no idea." But that was my reputation in the camp. When I said I was going to do something, I did it. They would often ask for things, and I would say, "I don't think I can help you with that, but I'll see what I can do." Sometimes, I could deliver for them, and they appreciated it. Overall, I had a really good rapport, whether it was getting people to confess war crimes or sharing secrets. Even in my daily life, as I network with people around the world, I can't tell you how many times, within five minutes of an initial conversation, people will say to me, "You know, I've never told anybody this before…" Even when I'm not trying to interrogate people, people trust me. I'm honored by that and respect it. It's kind of a sacred philosophy.

Chris O'Byrne:

I would imagine there's some natural skill involved that made it pretty easy for you to do so well, but what techniques did you learn? How can we apply what you've learned to meeting somebody at a conference and starting a conversation or other life situations?

Daniel Hammond:

My mom has a PhD in biochemistry. She's a very structured, logical thinker. I have that but without the fancy degrees. My dad is a people person. His field was training and development. I think natural aptitude helps a lot, but there are things you can learn. I taught interrogation. I saw some people who were horrible when they started but mastered the skills.

Age also helps. It was harder to train people at seventeen because they just didn't have the life experience. Much of it boils down to this: How can I connect with you? At this point in my life, I have done so many various things that most people can't tell me three things about them that I can't find a direct connection with something I've done.

The first thing is truly caring about people helps. It lets you connect with them when you are interested in what's important to them. That's the key. If somebody is not cooperating with you in interrogation, it's because you don't understand their motivation. What do they care about? If you slow down and take the time to evaluate what that is and connect it in some way to how helping you will help them, it's a pretty simple process and the more committed they become.

I ended up helping to design an advanced interrogation and analysis course for the military. The focus of that course was successfully and ethically interrogating those people who are incredibly committed to not being helpful. However, the process still involves chipping away at their stories and lies and getting to what they really care about. They will try to convince you that they care about certain things, but if you can dismantle that and get to what's below it, you can still reach that level of agreement. Again, it's a trust thing. You have to maintain your credibility throughout. As soon as I lie to you and you catch me in a lie, it's over. I find it's easier not to lie because that's taking up head space. It slows you down, and people know that you are hedging in some way, shape, or form. I like to speak the truth. I told one white lie in my nine months of real-world interrogation, and it was because I was caught off guard. I was asked a question I did not want to answer, and I hedged. They asked me if I was in the CIA or the Army, and I was an activated Army Reservist at the time, but I said neither. It was a lie, but it was not in my best interest for them to have that knowledge.

Chris O'Byrne:

How do you get below the surface-level stories they're telling that aren't the truth?

Daniel Hammond:

For most people, it doesn't take much. You just need to ask them what's important or explain a logical reason for why you need the information, and they'll start talking to you. Those hardened criminals—war criminals, terrorists, insurgents, or whatever they are—have effectively been programmed. They've been told things. One of the stories coming out of the First Gulf War, which is not my war, was they were told that Americans were going to torture them and be brutal to them. Then, we're like, "Hey, you want some food?" And they're confused, because often they didn't get food from their own military. Their leadership made gaining cooperation easy because we didn't do what they expected.

It's usually not that hard if they really hate you. It's a matter of deprogramming. You must find the flaws in their logic and start disrupting those. I believe that the truth is the key that unlocks all the doors. If they hate you, I say, "Well, I'm a soldier; you're a soldier. We're both trying to represent our countries to the best of our ability. How long do you want this war to drag out for your country? Because I'd like this war over tomorrow. If you don't help me, we could be here forever." Sometimes, it's just a matter of letting them realize, *Oh, yeah, he's like me.*

The values of cultures are very different. That surprised people more. I had more exposure to that than some of the people in the military. Once you understand their baseline of what matters in their culture, it's reaching out and caring enough to connect with them.

However, some things don't make any sense to me. The value of life in the Middle East is not

what we consider the value of life in the US. They talk about it more casually. "Oh, well, if I accidentally kill somebody's kid, my tribal leader talks to their tribal leader. They say, "How big is the check I must write?" And then we're good. For Western cultures, I think it is harder to let go of if somebody is responsible for killing your child. But it's a different culture. I'm sure everybody thinks their culture is the best culture. A lot depends on where you were raised.

Chris O'Byrne:

What led you into business interrogation?

Daniel Hammond:

I have a huge curiosity and an ability to quickly learn things and master them. One thing I encourage people to do, which served me well, is as soon as they get assigned a role, figure out all their responsibilities. Then, move outward from there. *Why do I do task A? Oh, task A serves this team over here.* Then, understanding what they need me to deliver will help me perform task A in an optimized way and better understand who they are and what they need so that as I run across opportunities, I can channel that to them.

Even in the military, I was the person that they would send to do the tasks no one knew how to do because I was like a fire-and-forget missile system. They just aim Specialist or Sergeant Hammond at it, and then, they don't worry about it because they know that I'll figure out how to check the box, what needs to happen, and make sure that everybody delivers what needs to happen.

However, eventually, I'll reach a ceiling where I have little more to learn. I know my job and the jobs of everyone around me and everyone I work with. Then, I feel stuck and start to look for something else. I was working for a top-ten global bank. I taught myself cyber threat intelligence. That was my third intelligence discipline. I went from self-taught to the lead analyst at the bank in three and a half years. Then, I was like, *Now what?* I trained my replacement. They were doing cyber exercises and designing scenarios. I was designing scenarios as an instructor in interrogation. I like building disaster scenarios and running people through them. Again, I got good at cyber exercising because I was good at identifying the needs of the executive we were serving, the needs of the cybersecurity perspective, and the needs of the business. Therefore, I could design an exercise to check as many boxes as possible for as many people as possible while delivering as much value as possible.

Eventually, I mastered that as well. I led an industry-level exercise for the financial services industry, where I facilitated an exercise in front of the US Secretary of the Treasury. Unless the president's going to come to an exercise, I don't know how much higher I can go than that. I always looked to maximize my learning opportunities each year. I always asked, "What's the biggest challenge for the team?" And I took on that challenge year after year. I continued to grow.

That's the key for me— continuous growth. I'm always looking for something new, something different. I took up bass guitar at age fifty and play almost every week at church. I like constantly saying yes to

challenging things. I volunteer in an inner healing prayer ministry because I got a lot of value from it. I help people sort out their past and find peace. I helped build a nursing school in Central Honduras with an amazing team. It took us five years to build the school. We raised almost a quarter of a million dollars and built a modern facility that serves nursing students and the local community with the clinic.

Making a difference is important to me. Somebody asked me recently, "What does success look like to you?" Success to me is being able to look back over my shoulder of my past

and see the people I helped and served. If I can give somebody a tool that helps them 10X their future, I want to hand out tools. That's why I love Business Interrogation. Many people know they have a problem in their business, but they're busy and don't have the time to explore what that is. Sometimes, that comes with a very high cost. If a team member disrupts the peace within your organization, you're paying a high cost for that. Just knowing or suspecting that there's somebody who needs to be gone does not make it easy. Sometimes, they have a critical role, making finding somebody to replace them more painful.

But again, for the good of your organization, you must take care of those things.

Sometimes, it's not being ready to get to the next level. Something is holding you back, a lack of systems or a lack of a key role. You need to turn over the finances to a financial officer, or your technology guy needs to stop worrying about all the technology and start leading the team of technology solvers. I see how things fit together and map those connections. I used to say I could break anything because I see where the connections are weak. I keep asking questions until I understand how all the pieces fit together. I don't need to know what the processes are. I just need to know how the connections touch and what's important in each connection.

I was once called a Swiss Army chainsaw, because I can usually come up with a solution for almost any problem. Explaining it is sometimes harder, because I see how things are connected more clearly than they do sometimes. I was once instructed to build a scenario I knew was not going to serve the people it was for. However, they insisted. Two months and 75 interviews later, the outcome was orders of magnitude greater than they thought was possible and they canceled the scenario, because it was far outside the risk tolerance for their leadership.

Chris O'Byrne:

When somebody asks why they should hire you, what do you answer?

Daniel Hammond:

"How important is your success to you?" is one of the questions I would ask. I find problems, anticipate problems, and find hidden opportunities. In the military, they say military intelligence is a force multiplier. That's what I am. Many companies have a visionary founder and then his COO, who makes it happen. I'm both of those things. I get the visionary thing and understand how to make it happen. I don't want to be in either of those roles. However, if you're trying to do something new, I can help pull that vision out of the visionary and add additional value to it, seeing some of the next-level things that can be done as you're building out that new capability. I'm also able to help translate it to the implementer so that they understand what they're trying to accomplish and what it will lead them to… connect them to the purpose and outcome. Sometimes, the implementer sees that the way they currently do business won't work with this new vision. Are you going to rip the company apart trying to make this happen? I can also translate the concerns of the implementer back to the visionary so that we can find a plan that doesn't risk

the things that they do well while we build out this new capability to the new vision.

Ideally, I would not be comfortable in a static role. I like new challenges constantly. When I started, I called myself a cybersecurity consultant, but I feel like I'm more of a strategic advisor. I ask, "What do you want to accomplish?" Then, I help you dream that into existence and get a blueprint for what it looks like.

When I started as an entrepreneur, I was a cybersecurity consultant. I designed fictitious but realistic cyber scenarios—effectively, fire drills for your network to help you think through what to do in a cyber disaster. Then, COVID hit, and I realized very quickly that nobody would hire me to build a fictitious disaster for them while they were in the middle of a real-world disaster. I took that opportunity to grow myself. I joined the John Maxwell team. I went through all of their leadership training. I started reading about personal growth, learning about running businesses, and how to be more effective with my time. I ended up also doing a contract for a major financial institution that qualified me for Dan Sullivan's Strategic Coach® program, which helped up-level my entrepreneurial thinking.

Everybody has a Unique Ability™ (owned by Strategic Coach),

and that's what you do better than anyone else. I love unique-ability collaborations. How can I take what I do and see how it energizes and synergizes with what you do so we can serve our clients in new ways?

One of the leaders on the board with me for the nursing school project was Dr. Ted Anders, and he had a system called Customer Driven Leadership™. He traveled all over the world for decades, helping organizations. He worked with visionary leaders to dream up the company they aspired to lead. Then his system gets that vision down to the lowest level of the organization, and inspires everyone to begin creating it from the bottom up. It starts with infusing people with your journey to build the organization and rewarding them through incentives when they help you achieve that growth.

I said earlier I could break anything. However, with Ted's Customer Driven Leadership system, I couldn't. I had never encountered a self-repairing system like his. Any disruption I could cause would show up in less than a month on a report showing where the problem was. So, we went into partnership. I became the managing partner and co-authored a book to tell the story about his system and a second one to help people install that system in their organizations. That's another thing that falls under that Business Interrogation umbrella, helping to balance Customer Driven Leadership equations to get your business where you want it to be.

Chris O'Byrne:

Is there anything specific that made Dr. Anders system unbreakable?

Daniel Hammond:

It might surprise you. It focuses on what is important to the customer. That's where you start. Then, you look at how you want to grow, a vision of the future. I'd say the next most important things are being clear, living your values, and having systems in place, because ad-hoc growth is limited. You can't get to the big business world without systematizing what you do. It should be a repeatable process, but it shouldn't be a static process. You should reflect on the systems you have in place and think about how to improve them.

It's also important to decentralize. There are some organizational operating systems out there that are top-down. I tell you what I want you to do. I tell my lieutenants. They tell their leaders, and they tell the next in command, but it's very self-directed. Things get lost in translation. When I tell somebody what I want, part of that is their interpretation of what I've said.

It's the telephone game. If you could hear what comes out as your directive at the functions furthest away from you, you might be shocked at what they think you wanted.

If everyone has clarity throughout the organization of the ultimate purpose, you'll achieve more. Then, everyone is making decisions based on helping us get there. Part of it is defining everyone's responsibilities and authority. If you have to cross one of these lines to solve the problem it needs to be escalated. No one but the most senior leader should have the authority to write a million-dollar check to solve a five-dollar problem. That's bad for business.

Additionally, you ask each team or function within the organization, "How do you serve the other functions?" And then you ask the teams you serve, "What's the one thing I can do to help you serve your direct internal client better or better serve the external client?" Then, you just work on getting better and better at that.

You're doing that 1 percent growth over every connection within the organization month over month. When you master that, you add the second most important thing. Then eventually the third most important thing. It's a system that empowers. Each function becomes an entrepreneurial problem-solving intrapreneurial unit. They're getting better and better at serving their internal clients, which helps you serve the external clients better. Everybody's evaluated by who they serve. Instead of the team leaders telling the worker bees, "This is how many stars I assign you for the work you have done for me over the last year" and maybe that comes with additional compensation or maybe it doesn't. In our system, team leaders commit to the team how they will serve the team better, and then they're evaluated by the team. Did they do what they said they would do to help the team succeed? The leader of the team and the team share a score. Seventy percent of their score comes from what they do together. The leader gets scored for how well they served their team and did what they said they would do. The team's 30 percent is about how they score each other. The team members are evaluated by two things: Where did you not live up to the organization's values, and where are you not a good team member? What are you doing that's hurting the team? That feedback comes to you. It hurts your score, but you know what to do to be a better teammate. It's constant improvement everywhere. It's the same with the leader; they know where they missed the mark. It creates a self-evolving system.

Chris O'Byrne:

That emphasis on teamwork now forces you to start thinking as a team member.

Daniel Hammond:

I completely agree. One of my favorite examples is a sales team. If you and I are on a sales team together, and I have a secret that helps me close 20 percent more sales, do you think I will share that with anybody else on the team? Probably not, because I want to be the best salesperson on the team. That's what will make me the best salesperson. When I go on vacation, will I hand over my lead list so you can start working on my leads? Heck, no. That's just the reality.

However, in this system, we're all scored together. Now, that 20 percent secret I have is something I want the rest of the team to have because when we're all more successful, we will get more incentive payments. This mentality helps everyone get better.

Chris O'Byrne:

What are some common problems or issues you see in businesses?

Daniel Hammond:

Many of them, especially small and medium-sized businesses, don't have enough systems in place. Another issue is a lack of clarity in how they serve their customers throughout the value chain. When you have that full picture, it changes everything.

One example is a production team leader who assumes that increasing production by 10 percent will help the company. So, they become a taskmaster and try to get their team to push out more and more without connecting and asking, "Do we truly need higher production percentages?" Because sometimes, when you start pushing your people, quality decreases. Maybe production increased, but you're getting more customer complaints, and your reputation is suffering. Or let's say they fill up the warehouse, and suddenly, they find a glitch or a bug in the system, and they have to fix it. They have all this bugged stuff they've created because they over-produced without thinking about the consequences. Therefore, having the systems in place where there's monitoring, and you're not producing stuff that the company doesn't need. It's one thing to plan for Black Friday or the holiday rush, but you must have a strategic plan and the systems to support that.

Another mistake is not investing enough in your people's growth and leadership. Coaching up to the most senior leadership is critical. Growth is vital, but there are a lot of ways to grow. You could be part of communities of entrepreneurs where you're cross-sharing information. You could hire a business coach who helps you create a strategic plan for your future. You could hire people to help you implement systems or focus on your communication challenges. You could implement a specific assessment for the whole organization, whether it's DiSC, Kolbe, Clifton-Strengths, or Why.io; there are many tools out there to help you understand each other and how to better communicate with each other. Any investments like those pay gold. They help your team feel like you're invested in their success, which increases their loyalty and fulfillment in being part of your team. We have a client who's been running CDL for over 25 years, and they said that they grew from nine people when Ted introduced the system to them to over 300. The company's CEO said they had a 20-year period where they only had five people quit to go work elsewhere. You find a place where they treat you with respect and value your contribution; who wouldn't want to work in a company like that?

Chris O'Byrne:

We often talk about hiring the right person for the right seat. We discuss the hiring process, ensuring we're hiring good people. However, I have seen where companies neglect to develop them. Sure, they need

to have the raw material of their character, work ethic, and some of those things. But I remember many times when I was in a position and wished somebody would have invested something in me to become better at what I was doing, which I know would have made me want to do even better because of that trust and concern for me. I'm glad you brought that up because I see that too often when it is a problem and not done correctly.

Daniel Hammond:

One of the other biggest mistakes I've seen is hiring from the outside when you haven't assessed the talent from within because then you're rolling the dice. You don't typically know what this person will bring. I competed for a role once when it was one of those corporate games where they already knew who they wanted to hire but had to post the job. Of course, they don't tell you, "Hey, you won't get this job even if you apply." I made it through four interviews before they finally went with the guy they were always planning to go with. But I did my research, had a plan, and knew how to drive that. The person came from the outside. They didn't understand our culture. They didn't know how everything worked. And I don't know that they accomplished much in their first year there, whereas I was ready to drive that train forward from day one. Then, how do I

feel? I know I'm competitive. I know what they want better than anybody they could be talking to. So, why am I not being considered for this position? Eventually, somebody admits they knew all along who they would hire. It destroys morale.

Chris O'Byrne:

What are some ways a business can improve?

Daniel Hammond:

I call it kicking the tires, which means having somebody ask you questions about what you're doing and how you're delivering periodically. That could be a coach or mentor, but it's at the senior leadership level. The CEO shouldn't be above learning and getting coached and advice. Even if you're a Fortune 500 company, you grow by investing in growth and learning.

Once your business is successful, if you just keep running the way you're running, eventually, changes in the market will disrupt you. You should be looking for ways to disrupt the market because then you're considering what could happen.

That was key in my cybersecurity work. Sure, everything's working now, but what if you get hacked? If you haven't thought through that and don't ask, "Is there a circumstance where I would pay a ransom to unlock my computer systems?" you're making that decision under the gun.

People often want to hire yes people or go-with-the-flow, don't-rock-the-boat people. However, if everybody in your company is afraid to rock the boat, you will run aground. You need people challenging you. Maybe your function within your organization is to ask, "How can we make things better?" Maybe it's asking your customers how you can improve. Your customers' needs change. If you're delivering to them today the way they wanted you to deliver to them five years ago, somebody else will find a better way to deliver.

One of the mistakes business leaders make is patching symptoms within their business instead of drilling into what's the root cause. Those patches are often more expensive than solving the problem. Great, you've made it go away for you at the top, but it didn't solve anything for people dealing with the problem. Again, it could be somebody who's a bad fit for the culture of the business, who's in a leadership position, destroying morale on his or her team and all the people they work with. It could also be a system that no longer serves and needs to be looked at again.

I will never be happy in a stagnant business. I'm a disruptor. *Success Secrets of Disruptors* is one of the books I've been a contributing author to. My chapter is "Let's Get Uncomfortable." Whether you're a business leader or in your personal life, do something new that challenges you. For me, once, it was picking up a bass guitar and figuring out how to play. Seek the deep process of meaningful growth.

Chris O'Byrne:

What is one of the things that you tell people to do? Let's say they're not even considering working for you, and they're just wondering what they should focus on.

Daniel Hammond:

I like to challenge entrepreneurs to ask their customers, especially the most important customers, what's the one thing I can deliver for you that if I get that right, you will never look for somebody else who does what I do? What does perfect success look like? What is the most important component of success for you?

Chris O'Byrne:

What kind of answers do you get? Not specifically, but what's the theme behind them?

Daniel Hammond:

Many business owners make assumptions about what their customers want without asking them, "What do you want?" If you hire me, for example, to do a cyber exercise for your leadership team, but I see that one person on the team, maybe even in the planning of the exercise, is toxic to the success of your team or the success of your business, do you want me to just ignore that? Or do you want me at least to bring that to your attention?

We must look for what else, what other; that's part of the interrogation business. If I ask you what your priority is, and you tell me. And I think, *Okay, that's all Chris cares about.* I haven't done a good job. I may ask, "What other priorities do you have, Chris?" And then you tell me two more. I must keep asking, "What else do you care about?" until I understand what success means to you.

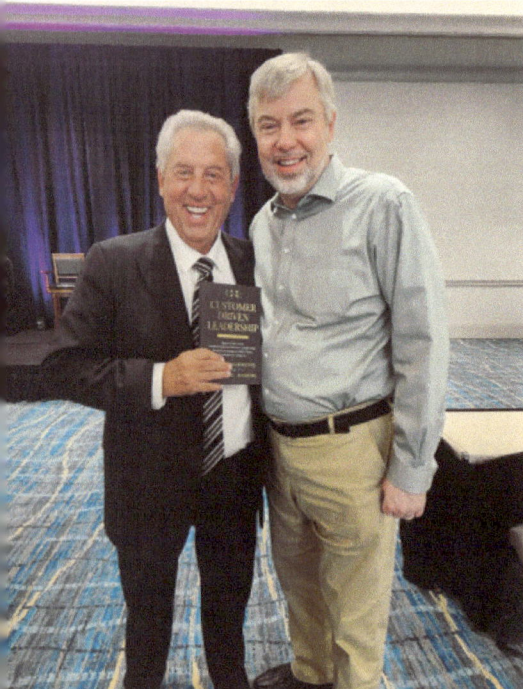

I often hear from business owners that they just lost their biggest client. Sometimes, that's great news. Maybe that's the disruption their business needs, but let it be because you chose that they were not a good fit or that you are serving other people in other directions, not because you weren't doing what they needed you to do. Don't get blindsided by that.

Chris O'Byrne:

Why do you do what you do in Business Interrogation?

Daniel Hammond:

For four years as an entrepreneur, I've been growing my network and meeting entrepreneurs worldwide. I care about them. I will often ask them because I care, "What's going on in your business?" or "What's the biggest challenge facing you right now?" Then, I'll ask questions about it. Often, they'll get clarity.

I once worked with an entrepreneur who had exited several successful businesses. They were creating a new business. I asked them five questions, and I broke their business model. Question five was, "What if your customers don't do that?" And they responded, "Oh, that would be bad. That would be bad." They solved that risk, and a month later, asked me to go deep with their process. The next time we

talked, we talked for two hours, and they had their entire process documented. They said, "Ask me anything." We went through their entire process, and I kept asking questions like, "What if this happens? How would you handle this? What if this occurs? What's your next step? Who would handle that?" They had at least seven to ten good "aha moments" in those two hours. That was probably the most fun I've had as an entrepreneur, and they left with greater clarity. All I did was ask them the questions and then they had to consider what the answers would be.

If I could, I'd do that for the rest of my life, and I'm not planning on retiring. For me, it's finding those right-fit entrepreneurs trying to change the world. I'd like to work with small or medium-sized businesses where I go in once a year and ask them questions and challenge them. Some entrepreneurs own five to ten businesses, and they're constantly innovating all over the place. I would love to be on retainer with them and on three or four calls a week with people like that who are creating meaningful global positive change. Entrepreneurs create value for the world, especially when they do it ethically, which most of the ones I've met do. By helping them be successful, you push back against chaos and dysfunction and make the world a better place.

Chris O'Byrne:

That makes a lot of sense, especially given the background of how quickly you learned and how quickly you got bored. You can't get bored with something like this because it's always something new: a new company, a new group of people, a new set of processes, a new model. How does somebody learn more about *Customer Driven Leadership*?

Daniel Hammond:

It depends on the level of understanding they want. If they want a summary, there are some podcasts where I go into pretty good detail on that. There's the *Customer Driven Leadership Legacy Edition* on Amazon and on Audible. Our website is CustomerDrivenLeadership. co (not .com). There's also a *Customer Driven Leadership Implementation Guidebook*. I would only recommend the guidebook for people who want to try to self-implement. If you plan to work with our team to implement, we'll provide those. It's a complicated enough process that I've mapped it out for people. Ted and I are the only people who can lead a CDL implementation effectively currently, but we have plans to expand. We have some CDL implementers in an apprentice phase we're developing.

Our focus remains: How do you plan to grow? Ted and I don't

want to travel worldwide for the rest of our lives. We want to teach other people how to do that. It creates more winning and more positive impact on the world. Therefore, we're looking to multiply.

You can also contact me on LinkedIn and tell me you're interested in *Customer Driven Leadership* or *Business Interrogation*. *Business Interrogation* will be my first solo book. I wasn't an author a year and a half ago, and I've already contributed to five books. I have two more in the pipeline. I will probably have seven books out in two years.

Chris O'Byrne:

If somebody is eagerly looking forward to the *Business Interrogation* book, how long do they have to wait?

Daniel Hammond:

I'm gathering case studies until the end of 2023. Then, I will build those into the book and share some real-world interrogation experiences and life lessons where I learned what questions to ask.

I'm a fast learner, but I'm a late bloomer. I'm constantly trying to improve how well I serve. I'm looking for businesses to interrogate now, so reach out on LinkedIn.

I am also always working on improving my process. It's a twenty-minute process. I'll set up a thirty-minute call to have a little pre-game and post-game analysis.

I had fantastic feedback from a client today. They said, "When I got on, I was really intimidated, but it was a gentle process. I learned a lot. The perspective helped." So far, I've asked everybody at the end of an interrogation, "How valuable is this to you?" because it's not about me. It's about others getting value out of it. So far, everybody has verbally affirmed that it was of high value. So, if you can use high-value analysis in your biggest business challenge over twenty minutes, take the time, and let's talk. BusinessInterrogation.com and BreakMyBusinessModel.com are places to learn more about how I serve in this way.

AI IN MARKETING: HOW TO OUTSMART THE COMPETITION

CHRIS O'BYRNE

In today's marketing arena, Artificial Intelligence (AI) is more than a buzzword—it's a crucial tool for outsmarting the competition. Let's explore how AI is revolutionizing marketing, from predicting customer behaviors to automating communications. I'll dive into the latest AI tools and strategies that are helping businesses gain a competitive edge. Join me as I unveil how AI is reshaping marketing and offering unprecedented opportunities to connect with audiences in innovative ways.

The Evolution of AI in Marketing

The journey of AI in marketing traces its roots back to the late 20th Century, when its application was in its infancy, primarily revolving around fundamental data analysis and the automation of simple tasks. These early implementations, though rudimentary, set the stage for the advanced systems we utilize today. In this era, marketers began exploring the potential of AI with simple customer data analysis, initiating automated email responses, and experimenting with simple recommendation algorithms in online retail.

The 2000s: Technological Advancements and Growing Adoption

As the new millennium dawned, the intersection of the rise of the internet and the advancement of digital technology led to significant progress in AI technology within the marketing sector. This period was characterized by a leap from basic functionality to more sophisticated data analytics. Marketers started to embrace enhanced customer segmentation and targeting, laying the foundation for personalized marketing. This era also marked the introduction of machine learning algorithms, setting a new direction for AI's role in marketing.

The 2010s: Mainstream Acceptance and Integration

The 2010s represented a turning point where AI became a central element in marketing strategies. During this decade, AI made its way into social media platforms,

revolutionizing targeted advertising. This period also saw the rise of advanced chatbots and virtual assistants, significantly improving customer service efficiency. Additionally, the emergence of predictive analytics began to offer deeper insights into forecasting market trends and understanding customer behavior. Using deep learning techniques further enhanced the scope of personalization in marketing strategies.

The Current Landscape: AI as a Driving Force

Today, AI stands at the forefront of marketing innovation, redefining personalization and efficiency in strategies. The current landscape is marked by real-time customer data analysis, enabling dynamic and responsive marketing tactics. AI's role extends to content creation and curation and sophisticated SEO and SEM optimization tools. Furthermore, integrating voice and image recognition technologies opens new avenues for enhancing user engagement.

The Future of AI in Marketing: Trends to Watch

Looking ahead, the future of AI in marketing is poised to be shaped by several exciting trends. Augmented Reality (AR) and Virtual Reality (VR) are at the forefront, blending physical and digital experiences to create immersive marketing that captivates consumers in

novel ways. Alongside this, there's an increasing focus on AI ethics and privacy. As personalization becomes more advanced, the balance between delivering tailored experiences and respecting consumer privacy concerns becomes crucial.

Another significant trend is the emergence of quantum computing. This technology holds the potential to process vast datasets, which could revolutionize predictive analytics in marketing. By handling complex calculations at unprecedented speeds, quantum computing could offer insights and efficiencies far beyond current capabilities.

Lastly, integrating AI with the Internet of Things (IoT) is set to enhance customer experiences further. By leveraging connected devices, businesses can gather more nuanced data to understand and meet customer needs in real time. This integration promises to bring a new level of interactivity and responsiveness to consumer engagements.

The evolution of AI in marketing reflects a journey from basic automation to sophisticated, data-driven strategies that are reshaping the customer experience. As AI advances, it promises to unlock new possibilities and redefine the boundaries of what marketers can achieve.

Key AI Technologies Shaping Marketing

Machine Learning and Predictive Analytics are revolutionizing marketing by enabling businesses to better understand and interact with their customers. These technologies utilize historical and real-time data to predict future behaviors and preferences. This leads to more targeted and effective marketing campaigns. For instance, businesses can easily tailor product recommendations based on a customer's purchase history and accurately forecast market trends and consumer demands.

Natural Language Processing (NLP)

NLP has become a cornerstone of modern customer interaction. It powers tools that offer seamless and intuitive communication with consumers. This includes chatbots that provide instant customer support and content generation tools crafting relevant marketing materials. NLP effectively bridges the communication gap between brands and their audiences with features like sentiment analysis to gauge customer opinions and feedback.

AI in Social Media

AI plays a transformative role in social media, especially in personalizing user experiences and enhancing engagement. It leverages user data to deliver highly targeted advertisements and employs sentiment analysis to monitor brand perception across social platforms. The impact of AI in this domain is seen in areas such as targeted advertising, which is based on user behavior and preferences, and in the real-time monitoring of brand sentiment and engagement.

Programmatic Advertising

Programmatic advertising, driven by AI, is revolutionizing the ad buying process by automating it and utilizing real-time data to optimize ad placements. This approach maximizes the effectiveness of marketing budgets and ensures that ads reach the right audience at the optimal time. The key advantages of programmatic advertising include efficient ad placement, real-time bidding, and enhanced ROI through data-driven decision-making.

Image and Voice Recognition

Technologies like image and voice recognition reshape customer engagement by creating more interactive and personalized experiences. They enable users to search for products using images or voice commands, making the shopping experience more intuitive and user-friendly. In marketing, these technologies are employed in visual search tools for product discovery and voice-activated assistants for hands-free browsing and purchasing.

AI-Driven SEO and SEM

AI also redefines SEO (Search Engine Optimization) and SEM (Search Engine Marketing) strategies. AI analyzes search engine algorithms and user behavior by optimizing websites and ads for better visibility and engagement. It continually adapts strategies for maximum impact, including automated keyword research and analysis and dynamic content optimization for improved search engine ranking.

These AI technologies augment existing marketing strategies and pave the way for a new era of personalized and efficient marketing. By harnessing these tools, marketers can understand their audience better and engage with them in more meaningful and impactful ways.

AI-Driven Marketing Strategies

AI has ushered in a new era in marketing, where personalized engagement at scale has become possible and remarkably efficient. Through sophisticated customer data analysis, AI empowers marketers to design campaigns highly specific to individual preferences and behaviors. This targeted approach significantly boosts customer engagement and loyalty, as consumers are presented with content and offers that align closely with their unique interests.

Dynamic Content Customization and Segmentation

Utilizing AI algorithms, marketing content—including website materials, emails, and ads—can now be tailored in real-time to match individual user preferences. This customization is a critical step in creating a more personalized user experience. AI's advanced segmentation capabilities also enable marketers to classify customers into distinct groups for more focused and compelling messaging.

Automated Content Creation and Curation

In content creation, AI tools have become adept at generating creative material ranging from articles and social media posts to video content. This automation significantly reduces the workload on marketing teams, allowing them to concentrate more on strategic and design aspects of marketing. AI assists in drafting initial content and plays a crucial role in content optimization, analyzing performance, and suggesting improvements or new topics based on audience engagement.

Leveraging AI in Social Media Marketing

AI has particularly transformed social media marketing. These platforms benefit from AI's ability to optimize content, schedule posts efficiently, and provide in-depth analysis of user engagement, all of which contribute to fine-tuning social media strategies. AI's predictive analytics can determine optimal content posting times for maximum engagement while providing valuable insights into audience demographics and behaviors.

Programmatic Advertising and Real-Time Bidding

AI has revolutionized the landscape of advertising through programmatic advertising. This approach automates the ad-buying process, including real-time bidding, where AI makes instantaneous decisions on ad purchases and placements based on user data. This leads to increased targeting efficiency and budget optimization as AI continually adapts and learns which ad placements yield the best returns on investment.

Predictive Customer Service

AI has also transformed customer service by introducing predictive capabilities. AI-driven tools can anticipate customer needs and issues, enabling proactive solutions and engagement. This forward-thinking approach

not only enhances customer satisfaction but also lightens the workload of customer service teams, offering personalized support recommendations based on past interactions.

Optimization for Voice Search

With the increasing prevalence of voice assistants, optimizing for voice search has become a critical component of AI-driven marketing. AI aids in understanding and integrating the nuances of spoken language, facilitating the creation of voice-activated content and the incorporation of conversational, long-tail keywords that align with natural speech patterns.

These AI-driven marketing strategies represent a paradigm shift in how businesses approach marketing. They offer unprecedented efficiency, personalization, and insight, enabling brands to connect with their audiences in more meaningful and impactful ways. As AI technology continues to evolve, so will the possibilities for innovative and effective marketing strategies.

Future of AI in Marketing

The future of AI in marketing is set to be dominated by even more sophisticated predictive analytics. Leveraging vast amounts of data, AI will provide deeper insights into consumer behavior, predicting not just preferences but also future needs and trends. This will allow marketers to stay ahead of the curve, crafting strategies that align perfectly with evolving market dynamics.

Integration of AI with Augmented and Virtual Reality

AI's integration with Augmented Reality (AR) and Virtual Reality (VR) is poised to create immersive and interactive marketing experiences. These technologies will enable consumers to visualize products in real-world settings or engage in virtual brand experiences, deepening the connection between customers and brands.

Ethical AI and Consumer Privacy

As AI becomes more ingrained in marketing, ethical considerations and consumer privacy will take center stage. Marketers will need to strike a balance between leveraging AI for personalization and maintaining consumer trust. This will involve transparent data practices and adhering to evolving privacy regulations.

AI-Enabled Hyper-Personalization

Hyper-personalization will go beyond basic product recommendations, with AI curating entire customer journeys based on individual behaviors and preferences. This level of personalization will aim to deliver a unique and highly tailored experience to each customer, enhancing satisfaction and loyalty.

Voice and Conversational Marketing

The rise of voice assistants and conversational platforms will significantly shift toward voice and conversational marketing. AI will be pivotal in optimizing content for voice search and enabling brands to engage customers through natural language conversations, both text-based and voice-driven.

Quantum Computing in Marketing

The potential introduction of quantum computing in marketing could revolutionize data processing capabilities. This would allow for handling complex datasets at unprecedented speeds, providing near-instantaneous insights and enabling real-time marketing decisions at a previously unimaginable scale.

AI-Driven Content Creation

Advancements in AI will further enhance its role in content creation. AI tools will generate high-quality content and adapt it to different platforms and formats, ensuring consistency in brand messaging across various channels.

Enhanced Customer Experience with IoT and AI

The Internet of Things (IoT) and AI will offer new avenues for personalized marketing. Connected devices will provide real-time customer data, allowing for more dynamic and responsive marketing strategies that adapt to user behaviors and preferences.

The future of AI in marketing is brimming with possibilities. These advancements promise to transform how brands interact with their customers, offering more personalized, efficient, and engaging marketing solutions. As AI technology evolves, it will continue redefining marketing boundaries, driving innovation and creativity in the digital age.

How to Implement AI in Your Marketing Strategy

Before diving into AI implementation, evaluate your current marketing strategy to identify areas where AI can have the most significant impact. Look for processes that can be automated, areas needing enhanced personalization, or where data analytics could provide deeper insights.

Setting Clear Objectives

Define specific goals for integrating AI into your marketing strategy. Whether improving customer engagement, increasing sales, or enhancing personalization, having clear objectives will guide the selection and implementation of AI tools.

Choosing the Right AI Tools and Technologies

Select AI tools that align with your marketing goals and are compatible with your existing systems. Consider factors like ease of use, scalability, and integration capabilities. Standard AI tools include CRM systems with AI capabilities, AI-driven analytics platforms, chatbots, and personalized content recommendation engines.

Data Collection and Analysis

AI thrives on data. Ensure you have the infrastructure to collect, store, and analyze customer data securely and efficiently. This data will be the foundation upon which AI tools operate, providing the insights needed for effective marketing strategies.

Pilot Testing

Start with a pilot project to test the effectiveness of AI in a controlled environment. This could be an AI-powered email campaign, a chatbot on your website, or a small-scale programmatic advertising initiative. Monitor the performance and gather feedback for improvements.

Scaling and Integration

Once the pilot test is successful, gradually scale the AI implementation across other marketing channels. Ensure that AI tools are seamlessly integrated with existing marketing systems for a cohesive and unified strategy.

Training Your Team

Educate and train your marketing team on AI capabilities and best practices. This includes understanding the tools, interpreting AI-generated insights, and making data-driven decisions.

Continual Learning and Adaptation

AI in marketing is an ongoing process. Regularly analyze the performance of your AI tools, and be open to adapting strategies based on new data and insights. AI algorithms learn over time, so continuous monitoring and adjustments are essential for optimal performance.

Staying Informed on AI Developments

AI technology is rapidly evolving. Stay updated on AI trends and advancements to enhance your marketing strategy continually. This may involve attending conferences, following industry publications, or partnering with AI technology providers.

Ethical Considerations and Compliance

Ensure that your use of AI in marketing adheres to ethical standards and regulatory requirements, particularly regarding data privacy and consumer rights. Transparent and responsible use of AI will build trust and credibility with your audience.

Implementing AI in your marketing strategy is a journey that involves careful planning, execution, and ongoing management. By embracing AI, businesses can unlock new opportunities for growth, engagement, and innovation in their marketing efforts.

Conclusion

AI in marketing has transitioned from a novel concept to a vital strategy for staying ahead in the competitive digital landscape. This exploration has highlighted how AI technologies like predictive analytics, NLP, and programmatic advertising revolutionize marketing. As AI continues to evolve, it promises even greater advancements, reshaping our approach to customer engagement and business growth. Implementing AI requires strategic planning, but the payoff is clear: businesses that embrace AI gain a competitive edge and foster deeper connections with their customers. In the dynamic marketing world, AI is not just an option; it's an essential tool for future success.

FAQs

Q1: How Does AI Impact Customer Personalization in Marketing?

AI significantly enhances customer personalization by analyzing large volumes of data to understand customer preferences and behaviors. This allows marketers to create highly targeted and relevant content, offers, and recommendations. The result is a more personalized customer experience, increasing engagement, loyalty, and conversion rates.

Q2: What Are the Key Challenges in Implementing AI in Marketing?

The main challenges include integrating AI with existing marketing systems, ensuring data quality and privacy, and the need for continuous learning and adaptation. Additionally, businesses often face the challenge of selecting the right AI tools that align with their specific marketing goals and the skill gap in understanding and managing AI technologies.

Q3: Can Small Businesses Benefit from AI in Marketing?

Absolutely. AI is not just for large corporations. Small businesses can leverage AI for various purposes, such as automating repetitive tasks, enhancing customer service through chatbots, and gaining insights from customer data. Many AI tools are now more accessible and affordable, making them a viable option for small businesses looking to enhance their marketing strategies.

Action Steps

1. **Implement AI-Powered Personalization:** Based on the insights about AI's role in enhancing customer experiences, you can start by integrating AI tools for personalization in your marketing strategy. This could involve using AI to analyze customer data for personalized product recommendations or tailoring your website's content to individual user preferences.

2. **Adopt AI-Driven Analytics:** Utilize AI-driven analytics to gain deeper insights into your customer behavior and market trends. By implementing tools for predictive analytics, you can make more informed decisions about your marketing campaigns, product development,

and overall business strategy, ensuring they are more aligned with customer needs and market opportunities.

3. **Incorporate AI in Customer Service:** Enhance customer service by integrating AI technologies like chatbots and virtual assistants. This will improve customer experience by providing quick and personalized responses and streamline your customer support operations, allowing you to allocate resources more efficiently.

JOIN
Achieve Systems

BECOME AN ACHIEVE SYSTEMS MEMBER TODAY!

Education
We help you get the tools to create a thriving business! It's turnkey, you can start NOW!

Marketing
We provide marketing guidelines but also plug you into our conferences, events and database

Community
We have a thriving community of entrepreneurs and business owners for you to collaborate, refer and partner with to grow and up-level your business!

WE WORK WITH ENTREPRENEURS, BUSINESS OWNERS, SPEAKERS & LEADERS!

CONTACT US OR REGISTER HERE: www.AchieveSystemsPro.com

www.ingramcontent.com/pod-product-compliance
Lightning Source LLC
Chambersburg PA
CBHW052053190326
41519CB00002BA/201